Cambridge Elements ≡

Elements in the Philosophy of Law
edited by
George Pavlakos
University of Glasgow
Gerald J. Postema
University of North Carolina at Chapel Hill
Kenneth M. Ehrenberg
University of Surrey

THE DIFFERENTIATION AND AUTONOMY OF LAW

Emilios Christodoulidis
University of Glasgow

CAMBRIDGE
UNIVERSITY PRESS

Shaftesbury Road, Cambridge CB2 8EA, United Kingdom

One Liberty Plaza, 20th Floor, New York, NY 10006, USA

477 Williamstown Road, Port Melbourne, VIC 3207, Australia

314–321, 3rd Floor, Plot 3, Splendor Forum, Jasola District Centre,
New Delhi – 110025, India

103 Penang Road, #05–06/07, Visioncrest Commercial, Singapore 238467

Cambridge University Press is part of Cambridge University Press & Assessment,
a department of the University of Cambridge.

We share the University's mission to contribute to society through the pursuit of
education, learning and research at the highest international levels of excellence.

www.cambridge.org
Information on this title: www.cambridge.org/9781009001311

DOI: 10.1017/9781009004619

First published 2023

A catalogue record for this publication is available from the British Library

ISBN 978-1-009-45439-1 Hardback
ISBN 978-1-009-00131-1 Paperback
ISSN 2631-5815 (online)
ISSN 2631-5807 (print)

Cambridge University Press & Assessment has no responsibility for the persistence
or accuracy of URLs for external or third-party internet websites referred to in this
publication and does not guarantee that any content on such websites is, or will
remain, accurate or appropriate.

The Differentiation and Autonomy of Law

Elements in the Philosophy of Law

DOI: 10.1017/9781009004619
First published online: September 2023

Emilios Christodoulidis
University of Glasgow

Author for correspondence: Emilios Christodoulidis,
Emilios.Christodoulidis@glasgow.ac.uk

Abstract: This Element looks first at the fundamental principle of modernity that is the functional differentiation of society and the emergence of autonomous, positive law. The careful architecture of differentiation, balance, and mutual performance between the legal, political, and economic systems is jeopardised with the hypertrophy of any one of the structurally coupled systems at the expense of the others. The pathologies are described in the second section of the Element, which explores how, under conditions of globalisation, market thinking came to hoist itself to the position of a privileged site of societal rationality. In the third section, we look at what sustains law's own 'reflexive intelligence' under conditions of globalisation, and whether we can still rely today on the constitutional achievement to guarantee law's autonomy, its democratic credentials, and its ability to reproduce normative expectations.

Keywords: globalisation, human rights, functional differentiation, autonomy of law, juridification

ISBNs: 9781009454391 (HB), 9781009001311 (PB), 9781009004619 (OC)
ISSNs: 2631-5815 (online), 2631-5807 (print)

Contents

1 The Differentiation of the Legal System

Functional Differentiation

The emergence of modern society coincides with the process of its functional differentiation. While the time of a definitive caesura between premodern and modern society is always going to be approximate, a significant historical shift, however gradual, marked the transition from stratified, hierarchical, premodern societies to modern differentiated societies. The modern era was thus coincident with the emergence of multiple, *differentiated rationalities* across the spectrum of society. When it comes to the institution of law, this took the form of a move away from the principle of natural law that structured the normative imaginaries of earlier societies and towards the enactment of positive legislation. This 'positivisation' of law removes it from its comprehensive embeddedness in the relatively static premodern normative order and installs a different legal imaginary resonant of the new democratic imperative of self-legislation, especially as ushered in by the American and French revolutions, and capable of adaptation to the new dynamism of market societies. A response to the emerging complexity of societies required a *structural* departure, one that, in law, introduced a new semantic of citizenship on the one hand, and on the other of individual subjecthood and freedom, responsibility and rights. This was a new vocabulary that pushed against a semantic of accepted authority. Of course, such a process of the displacement of an all-encompassing normative order was never going to be comprehensive, simultaneous, or uniform across European societies. In his hugely influential *Law and Revolution*, Harold Berman argued that significant levels of law's autonomy had already been achieved earlier, in the eleventh and twelfth centuries, and the move to elevating the significance of legal culture was pioneered in Europe and did not occur uniformly elsewhere (Berman, 2003). The positivisation of law is a response to the emerging complexity of modern society and, though more gradually, took hold also of the common law, marking across societies a departure from traditional sources of legitimation. This will be the subject of the next section. Remaining for now with the organising principle of functional differentiation, we see that while the new principle largely comes to displace the earlier ordering forms of segmentation and stratification of premodern societies, these previous forms of differentiation find a certain accommodation within the newly emergent context. Even comprehensive shifts are not clear breaks. 'The evolution of this highly improbable social order', suggests Niklas Luhmann, from whom we will take the lead in the analysis that follows, 'required replacing stratification with functional differentiation as *the main* principle of forming subsystems within the overall system of society' (Luhmann, 1986b, 318, emphasis added).

The great sociologies of the nineteenth century, for all their profound differences, take the shift from stratification to differentiation as central. For Marx, the autonomisation of law and of politics – the development of separate legal and political systems – falsely cleanses their respective logics from their embeddedness in social labour, 'elevating' them to an 'ideality' where they track nothing of the 'profane' realities of material practice except in distorted ideological form (see Marx, 1843/2000). For Weber and Durkheim, with law as paradigmatic instance and 'index' of social reproduction, the shift is described in terms of a transition to formal rationality and organic solidarity respectively. For Durkheim in particular, modernity was marked by a new configuration of the nature of the social bond into a type of solidarity that he termed 'organic', and correlative to a new division of labour and pluralisation of spheres of value. The differentiation has to do with the gradual autonomisation of spheres and logics of social action and the development of separate semantics for the differentiated fields, with their principle of linkage – 'solidarity' in Durkheim – largely reconceptualised in the process (Durkheim, 1893/1965).

It was Durkheim who perhaps most emphatically placed the question of 'the social' at the root of sociological inquiry, confronted it as a sui generis category irreducible to individual rationalities and structures of motivation, and, prior to them, to ask sociology's fundamental question: *how is social order possible?* One can discern the urgency of the question against the background of the centrifugal tendencies of modern society, the new mobility and the acceleration of possibilities of communication, the new division of labour and the weakening of the old forces of order, approximating ever so dangerously the threshold of breakdown – what Durkheim called 'anomie'. But to address sociology's foundational question – the question *how is social order possible?* – with Durkheim we need to take a step back from the precarity of the 'accomplishment' of functional differentiation to *what makes possible* that accomplishment in the first place. And at this point the question is radicalised if one approaches it as a question of meaning-formation: if one asks, in other words, how is meaning *generated* in these radically autonomous spheres absent the semantic resources that tied it to generally shared reservoirs of communal value and orientation, and to the cohesive social imaginaries of the earlier age? It is this radical question that allows us to pick up the thread earlier – 'upstream', as it were – from the questions of what normatively binds together our modern centrifugal differentiated societies. Upstream, the question 'what makes social order possible?' is constitutively tied to a prior question: 'how is communication possible?' And, of course, to take *communication* rather than *the individual* or their *action* as the primary unit of social analysis makes action – and the individual whose action it is – that which is communicated *about*. It is to Luhmann that we owe this key methodological innovation because it is he who founds his sociology upon the articulation of the two questions (1972), and it is he who approaches it as a question of radical self-reference or, later, 'autopoiesis' (1995a/1984). But this is something that we need to take more gradually.

Look at how this articulation of the two fundamental questions – let us refer to this articulation as 'double contingency' but postpone for now its more detailed explanation[1] – allows Luhmann a more radical claim than is conventionally associated with the theorisation of functional differentiation. Luhmann's suggestion that modern society *emerges as* (and only as) functionally differentiated is premised on the idea that meaning is first stabilised (therefore 'generated') according to systems that are located at the sub-societal level, a level where their separate rationalities form and consolidate. Here are located the differentiated systems of law, politics, and economics, but also those of science, education, religion, art, and so forth. A particular combination of function, performance, and reflection, as we shall see, defines the possibilities of 'observation', relation and connectivity, and functional and semantic reach for each system in ways that are insular, particular to, and definitive of each of them. As the overall complexity of modern society increases, reflexive structures organise the internal complexity of these separate and plural domains. For the theory of social systems, the emergence of functionally differentiated systems, including that of positive law, is understood as a question of complexity and reduction, in a way that allows specific contingencies to emerge for each system: around what is legal and what illegal in law, costly or beneficial in the economy, true and false in science, promoting of or detrimental to the common good in politics, and so forth. To put it summarily, the disciplining of the double contingency of communication is the *reduction-achievement* of social systems, and it is accomplished at the level of each functionally differentiated system. The combination of the two founding questions – 'how is social order possible?' and 'how is communication possible over time?' – opens up a domain as novel as it is demanding: the emergence and consolidation of communicative domains or spheres that generate meaning are contingent on processes of systemic differentiation, and the problem of complexity, and therefore the question of how social order is possible, is answered as a question of functional specification. This specification sets every functional subsystem apart as a system within an environment that contains all other systems. And its own difference each time is elaborated from within, a *self-reference* that unfolds in time and allows the gradual generation and

---

[1] The question of 'double contingency', or the question over the possibility of meaningful interaction, originates with Durkheim and is formulated as sociology's key question by Parsons. With systems theory it is confronted as a question of complexity and reduction.

consolidation of systemic 'logics', as we have been describing them. Let us visit a couple of key examples of this process.

One of the earliest, certainly most theorised, and perhaps most prophetic accounts of a reflexivity that develops as a *self-referential* exercise is Machiavelli's theorisation of the political system. In *The Prince*, Machiavelli invites an understanding of *the political* as a sphere that is autonomous and reflexive to the measure that political rationality is concerned with its own operation and aggrandisement. Machiavelli's advice to the Prince is how to hold on to and maximise political power, with no other *ultimate* aim – albeit the *salus populi*, territorial expansion, economic development, and so forth – except the consolidation of *power* in his office. All other aspirations are referred back to this organising premise. The thinking of politics as self-referential understands the relationship with other fields as external to it, while simultaneously developing its own internally structured form of reflexivity understood as a self-oriented process. Of course, such self-orientation, and the observation of 'self' and 'other' that it enables, changes along the historical trajectory, and we know from Foucault's exceptional analyses how sovereignty, initially obsessed with its own expansion, by the eighteenth century was gradually giving itself a new field in the form of *governance* that allowed political rationality reflexively to reorient itself around new projections of its proper subject and to develop appropriate semantics (biopower, discipline, etc.) along the way (Foucault, 2000). Foucault is right to invite us to think about these couplings amongst systems, instances where self-oriented reflexivity develops as a result of, and a response to, the demands of the management of complexity; but this gesture takes nothing away from the argument about a *self*-reference that renews itself through referring *outside* of it, in the case of the political system (that we are discussing), to the *economy*, to the truths provided by *science*, or to the stabilisation of normative expectations guaranteed by the *law*.

If Machiavelli is the theorist of the *political system*, the most famous argument about the generation and consolidation of self-reference as it applies to the *economic system* appears in Marx's devastating critique of capitalism in the three volumes of *Capital*. Political self-reference had, after Machiavelli, already found extraordinary new articulations in social contract theory, where Thomas Hobbes had provided his fascinating treatise on sovereignty in the *Leviathan*, which pivots on the self-referential move whereby the *constitution of political society* involves its *subjection to the political sovereign*. David Ricardo expanded this line of thought to the economy; as Karl Polanyi puts it, with his customary eloquence, 'Hobbes' grotesque vision of the State – a huge Leviathan whose vast body was made up of an infinite number of human bodies – was dwarfed by the Ricardian construct of the labour market: a flow of human lives the supply of which was regulated by the amount of food put at their disposal' (Polanyi, 1944, 164). To Ricardo's construct, Malthus will add the devastating 'law' of the 'threat of starvation' holding in check the population in terms of the means of subsistence at its disposal (Malthus, 1992/1798). Marx picks up the cue from Ricardo to provide the famous analysis of the production and appropriation of the surplus value of labour. But the key moment of self-reference – the autopoiesis of the economy, as it were – is at the level of the basic self-referential reproduction of the economic system: in this context, the social (and socially plural and diffuse) notion of *value* comes to attach – as *exchange-value* – *from the outset* to the production and circulation of commodities.[2] This strict coupling of social value–production to economic exchange allows the profound internalisation of all social questions to the logic of the economy, and thereby the generation and consolidation of economic self-reference. The process includes the subjection of all the key societal resources to the logic of the commodity. Polanyi (1944) famously describes the markets in 'nature', work, and money as 'fictitious' because, unlike other commodities, they were not produced to be sold, and the price mechanism triggers, at best, slow and in any case imperfect adjustments to the supply and demand of these resources, resulting in acute consequences for the functioning of society. And yet for all the difficulties and the threat of social dislocation, once all societal resources are subjected to the 'market system', the internalisation is complete, and, we might suggest, the 'autopoiesis' of the economic system is set on its tracks.

The *legal system* follows a similar trajectory in the direction of achieving its own self-reference in the gesture of closure, which is at the heart of all positivisms: *the law is what the law says it is.* Hans Kelsen's 'pure theory of law' provides the most profound articulation of this closure. Under modern conditions there can be no reference to other normative systems, albeit religion, community morality, and so forth, as *source* of legal meaning; instead, legal meaning is conferred only internally under the sign of validity. Such is the radicalisation of the autonomy of law as a functionally differentiated system of modern society. We will return to this in the next section. In the meantime, let us reiterate the key development that accompanies differentiation, which relates to the way in which *contingency* comes to insert itself in the space occupied by the older guarantees and displaced certainties. No God-given right to rule to direct the exercise of political power; no *jus naturalis* to undergird the administration

---

[2] As a result of this ingenious internalisation, the question of value could not thereafter be posed except as extrapolated from within the logic of exchange, attached to the commodity form, and thus inextricably linked to the operations of capitalism's self-reproduction. See Christodoulidis (2021, ch. 3).

of legal justice. Instead, a 'formula of contingency' is introduced to drive the operations of each system: *legitimacy* measures the plausibility of political communications, the response to *scarcity* the performances of the economic system, the approximation to *justice* the operations of the legal system. The 'contingency formula' allows each system (consistently and persuasively) to communicate about itself to itself (Thornhill, 2006, 82), and thereby to organise its self-reference. There is a key connection to be drawn here between law's autonomy and the question of justice. As far as the legal system is concerned, 'the idea of justice can be understood as a formula for contingency of the legal system' (Luhmann, 2004, 214) in a roughly equivalent way as 'scarcity' plays that role for the economic system. 'The system defines justice in such a way that makes it clear that justice must prevail'[3] and 'the system identifies with [justice] as an idea, principle or value' (214). The quest for justice gives the system of law orientation, guides its reasons, and informs its programmes: in a nutshell, it subtends and supports its function. In its legal specification, justice must achieve 'adequate complexity' to deal with an environment where justice claims abound,[4] and this 'adequacy' will be measured, as ever, on not a normative but rather a functional register, which means one that secures the system's optimal reproduction.[5]

Clearly a multitude of questions arise at these junctures, over all the key assumptions that set out law on the path of differentiation with its very own balance of closure and openness to its surrounding subsystems. Difficult questions over how complexity (and contingency) are managed by the law, especially under the accelerated procedures of globalisation; questions over the 'porosity' of the boundaries between the subsystems, especially given how tight their articulations and overlaps appear to be. This in turn invites a question over the relation between the legal system and its political and

---

[3] At the risk of 'performative contradiction' as the discourse theorists would have it. On this version of the 'necessary connection' between law and justice, see in particular Alexy (1989).

[4] Luhmann suggests that while the extension of the concept of *justice* spans a number of systems (legal justice, political justice, economic justice), its semantic content is tied to each system of meaning in different ways. In this formulation we have both opportunity and limitation. 'Opportunity' because it allows these systems to communicate around it and, in a crucial sense, also to measure their adequacy by it. And 'limitation' because the question of justice can only receive from within every system a functionally specific answer.

[5] As Thornhill explains it,

> Luhmann's view that the differentiation of function systems in societal modernity is accompanied, distinctively in each system, by a necessary positivization of social meaning and its communicative underpinning. ... In consequence, each system of society must autonomously articulate, and, from within itself, endlessly generate and positively reproduce the communicative preconditions of its own consistency and validity. In this, to be sure, Luhmann asserted that the autonomous self-foundation of positive social meaning is a systemic function. (Thornhill, 2012, 67)

economic environments. Remember that with modernity, no hierarchical order obtains amongst society's systems any longer; and that the 'heterarchy' of systems must be maintained if differentiation is to continue delivering its dividends.[6]

Whatever further can be said about those dividends, the differentiation of logics and spheres of action unfolds in a mutually supportive (if not constitutive) relationship with the rise of *capitalism*. Where under feudalism the means of value extraction involved a combination of political might (including the use of arbitrary violence), personal dependencies, local affiliations, and so forth, under capitalism the means of extraction of value are entirely economic. Of course, as a question of *performance*, the legal system supplies property title over labour and other means of production and sanctions the bindingness of the labour contract. But it is *economic* conditions that set the price for labour and secure and frame the processes of social reproduction. The functional differentiation of the economy allows markets to do all the work of allocating value across the range of resources and their possible uses, which supports and informs capitalist production: exploitation is organised on the platform of the economy alone. As Ellen Meiksins Wood argues powerfully (Wood, 1981, 80), bourgeois economic theory abstracts the economy from its social and political context, severing production from political control and participation. As a result, any notion of the political economy is collapsed into its market form and subjected to the veridiction of the price mechanism, in the name of differentiation.

The Positivisation of Law and the Function of the Constitution

We looked at the positivisation of law as a response to the emerging complexity of modern society. The coupling of the legal system with other differentiated systems in its environment introduces into newly 'positivised' law a responsiveness to collective self-determination, on the one hand, and on the other, a reorientation to the transactional nature of the demands of the economy. The key organising principles of modernity, democracy, and the market are thereafter set on their tracks and in tension.[7] The principles of coupling – of law to politics and to the economy respectively – become highly dynamic and selective at this point. In both instances 'law needs to mobilise highly fluid and iterable accounts of its validity and cannot allow itself to be constrained by

---

[6] This places onerous demands on the systems that must now retain their openness to their environments, only on condition of which they remain *relevant*, while at the same time maintaining their closure, the self-reproduction or *auto*poiesis, in the face of the very real, and increasing, threat of *de-differentiation*, which would mark the loss of their particular means of generating meaning.

[7] See Streeck (2014) for one of the most acute accounts of this collision.

externally derived principles' (Thornhill, 2016, 57). The developments mean that the undifferentiated normative systems that guided earlier societies in terms of an amalgamation of religious, moral, and legal norms gradually lose their hold on modern society, where the law sustains itself as a self-referential system of positive law, commanding its own resources of norm-creation, meaning-generation, and, since it departs from traditional sources, also of legitimation.

The modern tradition of thinking the *social contract* is highly suggestive at this historical juncture, as the justificatory basis of the law is linked, first in Hobbes and Locke, later in Rousseau and Kant, to the political system (in the theorising of sovereignty and the general will) and to the economic system (in the theorising of property). It is these linkages at the level of both its operation and its legitimation that equip law, to repeat, with a close responsiveness to democratic will-formation in its coupling with the political system, and in its coupling with the economic system with a new openness to the transactional requirements of market society. Specific semantics are forged within the communicative structures of law to accommodate this dual orientation, in its simultaneous reflection of collective (democratic) and individual (economic) priorities, in the categories of public law and private law respectively.[8] As the law withdraws to the formal side of social interchange, away from substantive moralities, the *normative thinning* can be understood as *functionally* necessary because the development marks an *immunisation* of legal thought from the contents of normative orders (religion, morality, politics) that might have threatened its legitimacy in the pluralist society. Now the law becomes differentiated from these sets of values, and its uniform extension across society aspires to secure the *inclusion* of all citizens. The reproduction of positive law, as pared back from particular normative orders and immunised against broader social dynamics and conflicts, guarantees the *function* of generalising expectations. And this *function*, performed uniquely by the law, is what underpins its *differentiation*. By withdrawing to the formal side of social interchange, the law becomes the guarantor of what Max Weber calls the *formal-rational* order of society. Law's *reflexivity* is tied to the reproduction of law under the sign of validity. Functional analysis offers the opportunity to see how reflexivity organises the internal meaning-processing achievement that we know as modern law, by navigating the forcefield of complexity, and in the process organising law as a differentiated, self-orienting, self-observing domain of reduced complexity. This is how Luhmann summarises it: 'Our definition of the concept of law can no longer be conceived of in ontological, but, instead, in functional, terms. ... It is precisely the *functional*

---

[8] Critical legal theory draws useful leverage from these antinomies. See Christodoulidis et al. (2019).

reference to congruent generalisation that enforces this non-identity under complex, rapidly changeable structural conditions of the societal system' (1972, 174).

A special role for the *constitution* emerges in this context, in organising the particular reflexivity of the legal system. It is suggested that the constitution provides the *reflexive structure* for law's self-organisation as a system *internally*, and also how it enables law's *external* reach to politics, economics, and the other social systems that law is called on to 'regulate'. It secures forms of coupling with these systems that maintain its congruence, and it navigates the operations of law in their midst. All of this involves looking at the constitutional achievement from the point of view of enabling law's differentiation, autonomy, and social function. We might usefully approach this question by returning to the American and French revolutions of the eighteenth century. In the constitutional texts that these modern revolutions bestowed, we can track with clarity constitutionalism's conceptual innovation. An innovation that consisted of holding together a political and a legal system that could no longer be identified with one another, subsumed to one another, or incorporated in some hierarchy under an overarching natural right to rule. For Luhmann, with the positivisation of law and the democratisation of politics under conditions of modernity emerges the *evolutionary achievement* of the modern constitutions (Luhmann, 1990b). At a crucial point of the co-evolution of the differentiated subsystems of law and politics, the democratic self-determination of 'the people' detaches from corporatist forms – guilds, class and regional alliances, and intermediate associations – and becomes coupled to the semantics of the nation-state and is given expression in state law. The constitution holds together the political and legal systems, mobilises 'self-reinforcing' dynamics in each system, that do not combine in a unity. Instead, it is their *articulation*, and their reciprocal exposure, that stabilises the respective domains.[9] At the same time, both systems are able to consolidate their respective semantics: key concepts – popular sovereignty, jurisdiction, representation, and so forth – provide the vocabulary with the help of which are structured both the self-organisation of each system and its outward reach. It is around this emergent constitutional semantics that democracy and law manage their self-reproduction under the aegis of the constitution.

The achievement of constitutionalism is harboured in the nation-state as the dominant form of political self-organisation. As Luhmann puts it, since the nineteenth century at least, the concept of the political has been understood almost exclusively as referring to the state (Luhmann, 2004, 363). The state provides the unity that supports the differentiation of politics and law as structurally coupled in

---

[9] In Luhmann's formulation, a legal text first fixes the terms of a political constitution, and with it there occurs, says Luhmann, 'a legal establishment of a political order [whereby] one saw the political order as a legal one' (1990b, 178).

the constitution, designating the territorial limits within which the exercise of sovereign power, or in Weber's terms 'the monopoly of violence', was to be contained. We will return to the nation-state later when we look at globalisation; for now, let us merely hold on to the form of political unity that it offers and that harbours the differentiation orchestrated by the national constitution.

When it comes to the (national) constitution, we can distinguish its operation in two directions. Firstly, in the direction of the legal system's *internal* self-organisation and of its own unity; secondly, in the direction of its *external* reach and co-ordination with the political and economic systems in its environment. In the first direction, what is staked is law's *autonomy*; in the second, external dimension, what is staked is its *differentiation*. Let us take each in turn.

The constitution provides the reflexive structure that organises the legal system internally and underpins its *unity* as a system. This means that it secures the reproduction of law over time as *one* system, gathering new elements into existing structures. The dimension of time is crucial here because, of course, law's temporal modality is constitutively oriented to the past, drawing on what is *already* deposited as source of law. Except that now law's control of time involves the attempt to contain and 'tame' the radical reorientation from the past to the future (from 'tradition' to 'progress') that modernity ushers in with its promise of continuous progress, the temporal accelerations tied to technological developments, the new possibilities of communication, and so forth. It is in this context that the constitution becomes a mechanism for controlling the contin-gency that breaks onto the scene, unrestrained now by tradition and the inertias of the old order. The attempt to introduce a constitutional semantic to express the new temporal modality does not come free of tensions and paradoxes. In the new constitutional ordering, openness to the future means that the law foresees its own changeability and controls it by placing all law under constitutional scrutiny. The priority of the constitution above all other law means that the constitution now positions itself as measure of the legality or illegality of all laws, expressed and deployed most overtly in the constitutional review of ordinary legislation. What is here captured along the dimension of time also extends to the other dimensions of the meaning of the constitution (social and material).[10] The constitutional achievement sustains productively the paradoxes that have animated and bedevilled democratic theory, albeit the 'counter-majoritarian paradox' of reconciling self-rule and law-rule[11] or, at more abstract levels, the paradoxes that attend the coupling of the antithetical 'constituent'

---

[10] Luhmann introduces the 'dimensions of meaning' (material, social, temporal) in the second chapter of *Social Systems*. For an extensive analysis of the dimensions of the meaning of the constitution, see Christodoulidis (2021).

[11] See indicatively Ackerman (1984).

and 'constituted' powers,[12] or the mutually undercutting logic of norm and decision. In each case, it is the democratic dimension of law-making, and its dynamism, that strains at its constitutional containment. The impact on the political system is staggering: the fundamental political distinction between ruler and ruled under democratic-constitutional conditions breaks the tautology 'I decide what I decide' with the democratic paradox 'I decide and am bound by what I decide', a formula that holds together in an improbable balance the legal and the political.

These are all fascinating apertures that animate constitutional theory today. But our own ambition is more limited. It is to focus on how the reflexivity of the constitution engages the careful hierarchies and orchestrations that together provide the architecture of a complex legal system that is both relatively autonomous *and* adequate to the function of resolving societal disputes and of providing modern society with stable normative expectations.

It is not only in the highly systematic expressions in continental legal theory that the constitutional order involves the interplay of levels of norms as organising the reflexivity of positive law. The claim that thinking about the constitution involves distinguishing between first- and second-order levels of norm-creation also informs the heavily pragmatic tradition of the common law. Here too one finds a concession to a basic form of systematicity. Famously amongst legal theorists of this tradition, HLA Hart's description of the law as 'the union of primary and secondary rules' involves the articulation of first and second orders. 'Secondary' rules for Hart are 'on a different level from the primary rules, for they are all *about* such rules' (Hart, 1961, 92, original emphasis). The importance of these rules lies in their relation to primary rules in such a way that establishes a legal *system*.[13] Secondary rules allow the recognition of primary rules as rules of the system: they thus perform the elementary *constitutional function* of establishing system-specific criteria of identification and selection of rules as *structures* of the system. They fold the system back upon itself through establishing criteria of identity, or 'recognition', including also rules of change that orchestrate how the unity of the system might sustain its identity over time. Constitutionality is here for Hart the condition of possibility of a legal system, and the supposedly notorious 'circularity' of the argument – that 'recognition' is effected by actors always-already 'recognised' as capable of granting it – is in fact the inevitable condition of any system that operates through self-reference. Systems, Luhmann

---

[12] See indicatively Loughlin and Walker (2007).

[13] Hart argued that the transition from more 'primitive' to more sophisticated systems is marked by the development of this second layer of norms, and that the articulation of layers, primary and secondary, is what accounts for the development of the legal system under the exigencies of – not his word – complexity.

will argue, 'exploit' such tautologies and paradoxes, turning virtuous what critics of Hart would see as a vicious circle; a point made already without the use of systems theory by scholars like Neil MacCormick, who argued that it is precisely that circularity that allows legal institutions to develop in relations of mutual support with political institutions (MacCormick, 1981).

If the articulation of levels grounds constitutionality as a condition of the legal system in Hart, in Kelsen's more elaborate account it underlies imputation, establishes constitutional recall, and grants validity, and with it 'objective' legal meaning to subjective acts that, in the process, are selected as elements of the system.[14] Note all that is delivered in the process: through what is selected out and granted legal meaning, the *contingency* of social and political life comes under law's control. The result is that law achieves *a binding of normative expectations*: certain expectations receive law's sanction, entrenching what the legal system remains committed to, and what it will submit to change, under what conditions. In the process, the constitution will provide the limit of *normative regress*, in the sense that the answer to the question 'what is the law that governs the case at hand?' can only travel back, by way of attribution and interpretation, to the meaning of the first constitution. That all this needs to be kick-started through the hypothesis of the *Grundnorm* in Kelsen, as we saw, at some deep level is an inevitable feature of self-reference that at some point must breach the fundamental tautology that it is law that validates law. Luhmann, for one, has little interest for that 'unnecessary' and 'unlikely construct' of Kelsen's; for Luhmann, law's positivity inheres in circularity, or the fundamental *tautology* of the legal system, as he describes it, that 'the law is the law because it is the law' (Luhmann, 2004, 168). Law's cognitive openness and its responsiveness to a changing world develop on the back of precisely that normative closure that underpins it *as* positivity, guaranteeing its independence from any 'super-regulative' instance like morality, discursive propriety, reason, or nature, and based solely on its own self-reference.

The self-description of the law as constitution makes it possible to condense and concentrate the self-reference of the legal system. In other words, the legal system turns its self-description 'as constitutional' into the accompanying reference of all its operations that claim to be a part of the self-reproduction of the legal system. The claim that all law is under the authority of, the

---

[14] It is an architecture that finds in Hans Kelsen its most profound expression. In Kelsen's sophisticated image, the complexity of norms at the various levels are held together through validity, conferred by superior norms on the norms they authorise, downstream all the way to individual norms (judicial decisions, individual legal actions), and upstream all the way back to the first historical constitution that authorises everything that it mandates as valid, and is itself held in place as a norm by nothing more than a hypothesis (the *Grundnorm*).

constitution is sporadically tested in constitutional cases, though for the most part it runs silently alongside the operation of the system, that through reflexion now closes the circle of self-reference because only what is constitutional is legal. Constitutionality gives the system closure, and contains its centrifugal tendencies and the pressure towards variation by condensing its semantics, consolidating constitutional value, and securing re-iterability. The function of rationalisation, formal and distinctively legal, is thereby performed.

The account of law's complex positivity would need to be further developed fully to capture what is *autopoietic* about it, but perhaps enough has been said to establish the important first premise of our analysis as it relates to how the legal system organises itself. But if what we have called 'reflexivity' organises the legal system's unity *internally*, the law must simultaneously refer to situations *outside* of it, in politics, in the economy, in education and housing policy, in culture and family life, with regard to social conflicts and social demands. Such reference allows the law to keep pace with society whose normative expectations it is its function to regulate. And it is this that takes us from the internal register, in which reflexivity organises the *ratio juris* as it were, to the external register, on which the (horizontal) relation of law to other systems is managed as a question of *performance*, and on which the (vertical) relation with society is managed as a question of *function*. In other words, where reflexivity turns the law inward to reflect on the proper operation and attribution of legality, performance and function turn it outward to the distribution of legality to acts in the world; function describes the relation of law (as with each functionally differentiated system) to the overall system of society, and performance describes the inter-systemic interface with other subsystems.

Performance is the term that captures the contribution that one functional subsystem makes to the self-reproduction of another. We explored this already with regard to the legal and political subsystems. In their reciprocal cross-reference across the systemic boundary, systemic communications couple around common concepts but meaning-construction is always, and could only ever be, internal. Reference to each other (*hetero*-reference) relies on projective vocabularies, signifiers that travel between the systems, only to become aligned, upon arrival as it were, to the co-ordinates of the receiving system. To secure this 'coupling' each of the two systems need to adapt and organise their own semantic resources *adequately* so that expectational structures can be reproduced in a stable rather than random manner, although their own projective vocabularies, sensors and activations can only ever *approximate* other systemic constructions in their environment. The constitution sustains a coupling between law and politics that is reproduced over time as productive to both systems; 'improbably', we might add, because it demands that each system adjust its own internal complexity adequately across the systemic boundary with a system in its environment that it can neither control nor predict. The form of coupling that as part of the performance of each system secures the stable reproduction of both, is called 'structural coupling'. With 'structural coupling' a functional system can take certain structures in its environment for granted and rely on them. Take the example of such a coupling on a continuous basis between law and politics, such that finds its locution in the constitution, and look at how productive it is for both systems. The legal system impacts on the function of the political system, which is the reproduction of society through *collective decision-making* processes, decisions taken against the background of conflictually held positions, and grants legal sanction to such processes. At the same time the legal system relies on the political system (amongst others) to furnish (collective) conflict perspectives that will allow it to fulfil its own function of generalising normative expectations across society. Both systems depend on each other and must presuppose certain cognitive and normative structures as key to their functioning, which they cannot themselves produce. The lasting forms of structural coupling sustain 'performance' at these junctures.

An analysis of law's autonomy as a differentiated system needs to be complemented by an account of its *function* in society. That is because functional differentiation presupposes as a matter of conceptual foundation that each differentiated system performs a *unique* function. If two systems were committed to the same function, if in other words they were functional equivalents, then they could not be *functionally* differentiated. Which presents as a matter of first necessity to determine, delineate and delimit the function proper to law. And while the precise definition of law's function will be a matter of dispute, it would be relatively uncontroversial to gather the variety under some version of the 'rule of law' formula: the law is there to generate, to reproduce, and to guarantee relatively stable normative expectations for social actors in the face of the increasing complexity of the modern world and the rapid and widespread pluralisation of values. Unlike cognitive expectations, normative expectations are those that are held on to when they are disappointed.[15] While the occasion of reproducing these expectations depend on occasions of disagreement and conflict, an expectation is legal when equipped with the (second-order) expectation that it will be upheld on occasions when it will be tested, now and in the future.

---

[15] For the key distinction between cognitive and normative expectations, see Luhmann (1972). My cognitive expectation that the train I have bought a ticket for will arrive at a designated time will be discredited if it is disappointed when the train is late. On the contrary, my normative expectation that I am due compensation for the lateness is not discredited even if disappointed should the compensation not readily be offered.

The emphasis on the autonomy and the differentiation of law goes some way towards upholding the integrity of law, understood more broadly than the way that Ronald Dworkin popularised the term,[16] as what grants the distinctiveness of the *ratio juris*. Something more needs to be said about this distinctiveness and the integrity it upholds, which in turn points to a deeper justification of differentiation that those usually offered. Let us follow a different thread of argument in order to recover – finally in this section – the more profound defence.

An important discussion relevant to the positivisation of law under the aegis of the constitution, relates *differentiation* to what Jürgen Habermas has eloquently and influentially advanced in his later work as the *co-implication* thesis (Habermas, 1995, 2001). With systems theory we have seen that the constitution sustains a coupling between law and politics that is reproduced over time as productive to both systems. But the coupling involves a continuous interface between two systems that relate to each other only across a systemic boundary, which means that each system remains forever an environment for the other. Co-implication, on the other hand, names an articulation altogether more direct. Habermas uses the term to name a certain 'co-originality' and mutual facilitation between democracy and the law, a corrective, on the one hand, to the tendency (typically from critical theory) to detach democracy and constituent power from its reduction to constituted power, and, on the other, a corrective to the tendency (typically from liberal theory) to subsume democracy to rights and to the 'juristocracy' of the courts. Against Habermas' solution of the suggested co-implication of democracy and constitutional rights, or any dialectical articulation between them, Luhmann's account of the articulation of law and politics is only ever activated from the side of one of the two systems, law and politics never co-implicated but only asymmetrically 'actualised' from the point of view of either of the two rationalities. That is not to say that, for Luhmann, there is no account of the underlying unity; the simultaneous reference to the self and to the other, to system and environment, makes possible the observation of that which spans self- and other-reference, but only as the unity of their difference. The projective constitutionalist vocabulary means that what is referred to as constituent power is never more that the unfolding of self-reference of the constituted, never more, that is, than its 'accompanying reference'. It is crucial for Luhmann that '[s]elf-referential systems acquire information with the help of the difference between referring to self and to something else [i.e. their 'accompanying' reference] and this information makes possible their self-production'

---

[16] In *Law's Empire* (1986). There remains an unacknowledged, and potentially productive, overlap between the way in which 'integrity' balances the requirements of 'justification' and 'fit' and law's commitment to maintain justified normative expectations in the face of disappointment of those expectations.

(1995a/1984, 448). It is what secures for social subsystems that they have an outward reach; and for the legal system the opportunity to unfold the unproductive self-reference drawing everything inward and that would otherwise lock the system into the tautology that expresses what is quintessential in formalism, the thesis that the 'law is what the law says it is'.

The Role of Human Rights

The functional differentiation of modern society and the emergence of the semantics of fundamental freedoms and human rights are parallel and *complementary* historical processes. This is Luhmann's argument in *Grundrechte als Institution*. The entrenchment of fundamental rights protects society from the threat of regression into de-differentiation, because their function relates to the maintenance of autonomous societal spheres and facilitates the inclusion of individuals in all of them. For example, rights of contract, of exchange, and of property sustain the autonomy of economic practice, rights of academic freedom sustain educational practices, rights of access to courts and due process sustain the practice of law, and so forth. Fundamental rights, in other words, become the devices through which modern differentiated society secures the inclusion, liberty, and equality of its citizens by way of securing their participation across the range of its functional domains. As constitutionalised, they equip citizens with specific institutional capacities to have their rights enforced and acted upon by courts. Human rights become institutionalised in law in a way that reproduces them for the whole of society and, at the same time, sustains its internal differentiation. The particular threat that Luhmann had in mind here was the convergence of societal demands on the political system in a way that might lead to over-inclusion and de-differentiation, an attack, as far as law was concerned, on regulatory inflation that he indefatigably renewed. Constitutional rights offer the mediating structure that secures the 'relatively uniform' application of power in society, mediating in other words the centripetal tendencies of the political system and the threat of the regulatory state that Luhmann, in line with Hayek, warned against.[17] Like all 'structures', rights are self-descriptions of the legal system, which when properly functional allow stable forms of coupling between the legal system and the systems in its environment.

Let us stay with Luhmann's key emphasis on the new dynamics of inclusion, freedom, and equality that fundamental rights deliver. The normative meaning of functional differentiation, as institutionalised, plays out across all three

---

[17] See Section 2 below. Luhmann's *Political Theory in the Welfare State* (1990a) and *Ecological Communication* (1986a) took shrill tones in his attack on these grounds.

registers. Take each in turn. Rights achieve *inclusion* that is 'partial' and 'multifunctional': *partial* because it concerns particular aspects of one's individuality (citizen, legal subject, seller and consumer, churchgoer, pupil, etc.) and *multifunctional* because it traverses systems as the individual is only *transitorily* located in any one of them. The transitory nature of the individual's embeddedness in any one context, 'the indestructible possibility of moving from one thing to another', realises inclusion and freedom *in tandem* in the key idea of *passage*. That is because *freedom* is understood as unimpeded participation in the autonomous fields. And if freedom is to be thought of as a right to access to these domains, *equality* as guaranteed by fundamental rights means that one's social status neither qualifies one for, nor impedes, inclusion: all subjects are equally entitled to rights and protections.[18] The fact that one is poor does not impede one's right to education, that one is uneducated their right to access to the law, and so forth. The self-presentation (a key concept in *Grundrechte*) and mobility of individuals is guaranteed by the institutionalisation of human rights in a way that is essential to social *recognition*. They are protective of the 'symbolically-expressive dimensions of free action . . . and are concerned with the general right to free development of the person' (1965, 79). In the analysis of human rights, dividends of functional differentiation connect to the gains in complexity and autonomy. Fundamental rights carry those gains over to the concept, and self-understanding, of *agency*.

And yet, for all Luhmann's acclamatory endorsement, these are fraught processes, and they carry significant limitations. His own analysis is alert to at least part of this, and he appears somewhat anxious that the *objective* societal function that the legal system, for example, is called to sustain must rely on the *subjective* motivations and opportunities of individual rights-holders to raise and pursue claims before courts.[19] Questions of opportunity are particularly pertinent here, because access to justice, opportunities to raise a legal claim in court, place sometimes heavy entry costs that weigh down – if not compromise – 'inclusion'. But there is a second, weightier problem to which Luhmann's analysis pays scant attention. It is that the gains in functional differentiation delivered by fundamental rights involve a 'thinning' of those fundamental ideals – of inclusion, freedom, and equality – in order that they may be achieved. This is a deficit that Luhmann is happy to concede as merely a postponement of

---

[18] For secondary literature on Luhmann's analysis of human rights, see in particular Verschraegen (2002) and Guibentif (2016).

[19] 'Subjective rights guarantee that it is up to individuals whether they decide to make use of their rights or not', high entry costs and social pressures 'encouraging the non-participation of those they are meant to empower' (Luhmann, 2004, 418, 419). On this point see also Verschraegen (2006, 101).

a fuller realisation.[20] But an honest reckoning must confront both what is gained and what is sacrificed.

Take inclusion: functional differentiation marks a significant, and empowering, departure from societies where inclusion involved membership based on status, kinship, or locality, with all the attendant hierarchies, dependencies, and exclusions. Luhmann's introduction of the concept of 'exclusion individuality' at this point locates individuality at the cross-section of two axes (1995b, 237). On the axis of inclusion, human rights are the entry-points of participation; rights offer an all-inclusive semantics of universal and inalienable entitlement. On the axis of exclusion, individuality is what stands beyond the necessarily selective perspectives of function systems, signifier of what remains outside 'all the inclusions of the individual'. Individuals cannot but partially be included within society's function systems. This partial inclusion depends on systemic attributions, semantics of agency, the furnishing of speaking positions – all of them specific to each system. Self-reference, as we have described it, takes hold to equip agency with specific, contingent, and variable opportunities of individuation and address of subjects, to make sense of inclusion in highly selective ways. The 'excluded' subject then becomes included in a variety of registers, in each case drawing on system-specific thematisations and programmes, but in each case positioned at arm's length from any one of those contingent – never constitutive – associations.

The effects of the highly selective inclusion are felt most keenly on the issue of *recognition*. The differentiation of domains of action in which the individuals invest destabilises the mainstays of belonging and identity formation. Previous forms of differentiation typically granted persons status (albeit within highly hierarchical formations), all-embracing ties, and embeddedness. Functional differentiation by extending the framework of action across differentiated terrain deprives persons of the means of stable orientation and, crucially in this context, the means of self-presentation. If inclusion is thus effected largely at the expense of recognition, or at least of a significant shift away from its more stable forms, the cost will be felt at the level of the thinning of solidarity, which Durkheim had already described as a move to an 'organic' form that crucially – a point that Durkheim insisted on but was later largely lost – is *not experienced* by those partaking in it *as solidarity*.[21] The concept of solidarity in 'organic

---

[20] 'The inclusion of the population in society has to take a new form and this wish is framed in the form of subjective rights, because it is not realised yet' (Luhmann, 1989, 84).

[21] In the end, Durkheim himself will acknowledge the devastating effect of this question, as André Gorz reminds us too, when in the process of describing the subdivision of tasks he writes: '[T]he functional integration of individuals will prevent their social integration, ... and will exclude their forming reciprocal relations based on co-operation, for the purpose of achieving common

solidarity' captures the uncoerced process of social integration, uncoerced to the extent that it detaches from binding 'status' attachments and is floated instead in the spontaneous plural practices of modern societies, and uncoerced also because it appears legitimate as consonant with forms of motivation of market participation. But, of course, the term solidarity overstates those instrumental attachments, and Durkheim is conscious of that, although the loss never takes in his work the tenor that marks Weber's melancholic, disenchanted later analysis of this very transferral, in the rise and dominance of means–ends rationality (Weber, 1946).

Back to the expansive dividends that Luhmann attaches to functional differentiation: the effects are not felt solely on the register of inclusion; functional differentiation similarly involves the generalisation of a *thin* concept of both freedom and equality. Freedom is unimpeded participation in the autonomous fields; equality means that one's social status neither qualifies one for nor impedes inclusion: all subjects are equally entitled to rights and protections. The self-presentation and mobility of individuals is guaranteed in the institutionalisation of human rights, in a way that is essential to social recognition. They are protective of the 'symbolically-expressive dimensions of free action ... and are concerned with the general right to free development of the person' (1965, 79).

There is of course in this no pretence that equality will go anywhere beyond the most formal of conceptions, the guarantee that no institutionalised discrimination will prevent access to all citizens. In this classic gesture of abstention, typical of formal equality, *substantive* equality as relating to the meeting of social needs is relegated to subsystemic status and handed over to the economic system. The answer to complex equality is answered as a question of liberty (equal access to all systems) and differentiation (its demands too complex to be handled at the societal level). The meaning of social rights is thinned in line with the formal conception of equality as conceptualised independently of needs, or at least not constitutively oriented to meeting social needs. For Luhmann, instead, the currency of social rights is intimately tied to the logic of recognition-as-mobility; even the right to work is only ever referred to as the free choice of employment, where 'choice is free and exit is possible' (1965, 91) and free access to a variety of professional roles (131). Any other, fuller, needs-driven concept will be rebutted as incursion and a signal of de-differentiation, as a sign of a political system's encroachment on the economy and the 'absolutizing its own perspective'.[22] This metalevel gesture is devastating to the efforts of

---

objectives according to common criteria. Their organic solidarity does not exist for *them* as a lived relationship. It only exists as such for the outside observer' (in Gorz, 1989, 43).

[22] Verschraegen (2002, 272) in sympathetic mode.

a society politically to respond to its citizens' needs, as we shall further elaborate in later sections.

Let us take from this another important point about the way in which the *semantics* of subjective human rights dovetail with social *structures*, in this case the communicative openness of society and the role-structures through which people participate in its multiple functional spheres. In Parsons' complex categorisation (1937), the 'social system' constitutes an institutional order of interaction, an ensemble (structure) of roles organised on the basis of normed expectations and sanctions. Importantly for Luhmann, the institutionalisation of human rights as sanctioned (normed) expectations involves the self-limitation of politics, its containment in, and withdrawal into, its own *proper* domain. Moments of both inclusivity and exclusivity are achieved *in tandem*, rights acting to accentuate the positive inclusivity of the emergent political system of modern society, on the one hand, and, on the other, to 'exclude some spheres of social exchange from the purview of the political system altogether', 'acting to police the boundary between the political system and its social environments' (Thornhill, 2018, 363, 364).

If the constitutionalisation of fundamental rights carries this ambiguity as constitutive of what it means for law to be a reductive achievement, a reduction that we have described previously as a 'thinning' of the concepts of inclusion, freedom, and equality, it is nevertheless a clear guarantee of societal differentiation. On each of these registers, for Luhmann *de*-differentiation would impose unacceptable costs by upsetting the careful architecture of function and performance that holds the autonomous domains of modern society apart and linked. State overreach, so dreaded by political and economic liberals, is kept in check through actionable rights against the state, as are any excessive regulative gestures of the political system interfering with economic activity, educational practice, family life, and so forth, whatever the societal field of intervention. Rights thus sustain functional differentiation by keeping subsystemic rationalities within the proper limits of their respective domains of action.

Human rights law institutionalises the self-limitation of each sphere, and in that the legal system (in which such rights are articulated and sustained) grants itself a further function of policing the boundaries of systems and upholding the mutual demarcations. In another, later attempt to reserve a function for law as guarantor of differentiation, rights will be theorised as means to police the excessive growth impulses of subsystems, as Gunther Teubner will put it (Teubner, 2006), and the inevitable overstepping that that would involve. Let us add here that Luhmann is not alone in expounding the dividends of differentiation. Theorists from the liberal left have also warned against not taking differentiation seriously enough and have, if somewhat more reluctantly, attempted to draw some leverage for the theorisation of equality from differentiation (see Walzer, 1983).

Conclusion

It is perhaps time to gather together some of the lines of argument so far and summarise the question of the differentiation of the legal system, with all the dividends, risks, occlusions, and blind spots that attend it because general points arise for us from all the above attempts to tie the promise of justice to functional differentiation. If you run the differentiation of systems alongside Marx's critique of the continuous nature of capitalist exploitation, as it is organised, policed, and reproduced in the name of freedom, inclusion, and equality, they come to look a great deal like *enclosures* that fall neatly alongside capitalist distributions. Their differentiation inflicts a disarticulation, a containment of struggle within and as appropriate to the stake at hand, which carries over to the logic of action, saddling it with a partiality that it cannot possibly shake off because, like all successful ideological moves, it co-opts it *ab initio*. It is what sets capitalism on its tracks, driven by its own laws of motion.

On the other hand, and for all the caveats, limitations, risks, and occlusions, significant *dividends* do accrue from differentiation. It allows a clearer diagnosis of what the nature of the challenges of modern society are, and it warns against generalising perspectives across systems or spheres, where a certain logic of action may misread or violate communicative domains that are structured in ways that prevent the transferral of meaning across borders. Our analysis has tracked how meaning is generated at deeper levels, where different, partial rationalities emerge to cope with the increase in social complexity, and where linear, unidirectional, or uniform solutions are inadequate or dangerous. Where functional differentiation names a *heterarchy* of systems and logics of action where previous forms of differentiation installed *hierarchies*, dangers attach to the generalisation of one, single logic of action – political, economic, scientific, legal, and so forth – to the detriment of others, in a way that the resultant asymmetries might lead to the subjugation, displacement, or substitution of those other, variably differentiated fields.

For the rest of this Element, we will explore these asymmetries. Departing from the differentiation and functional specification that lay at the heart of the integration of complex society as we described it, we look at the asymmetries that install themselves at the junctures of the three social subsystems at the centre of this analysis: the legal, the political, and the economic. The expansionist tendencies of each of these systems, at the expense of the differentiation that held them together and apart, will be explored in Section 2, under the headings of 'juridification', 'politicisation', and 'marketisation'. Each of these terms names the expansionist trajectory of one of the subsystems at the expense of the others; it marks a pathology in the field of their performance, and consequently also a move against proper boundaries. Then we will move in Section 3 to look at how these asymmetries have been accentuated under conditions of globalisation and what, if· any, solutions might be offered.

2 Asymmetric Developments: The Spectre of De-differentiation

Juridification

The term juridification denotes not simply the exponential growth of legal regulation but more significantly its impingement on other fields. We can imagine juridification as having both horizontal and vertical dimensions. *Horizontally*, we can observe that in modern society law spreads its regulatory reach across an increasingly diverse range of social activities. It spreads, for example, into areas that were formerly considered private and beyond the proper reach of the law, such as aspects of domestic and family relations; and it spreads increasingly – though incompletely and unevenly – into the political realm. In each of these realms, legal norms gain prominence as a means of organising factual and normative aspects of social relations, which were previously under- or unregulated by law. The *vertical* dimension concerns the ways in which legal norms not only tighten their hold on already or newly regulated areas through increased legislation or judicial activity but do so by way of increasingly detailed normative standards. That is, rather than legal standards being general principles of reasonably broad coverage, there is an observable tendency for these standards to become more detailed in their specification of the factual circumstances that are being legally regulated, a phenomenon that is observable across a broad range of areas of legal practice.

The discussion of juridification connects and expands Max Weber's famous discussion in *Economy and Society* of the 'materialisation of formal law' (1978, 653ff). The modern state, for Weber, had initially departed from the corporatist nature of previous societies to develop an apparatus for the exercise of power in an a-personal, universal, and consistent manner, which he uses the ideal type 'formal-rational' to denote. However, Weber identified a later tendency away from the 'formal' and towards alternative types of legal formation, a tendency that was to accelerate as legal regulation turned to substantive provisions, which in turn led to the differential application of law to different categories, an increasing 'particularisation' of law, and the compartmentalisation of general standards into piecemeal, targeted regulation. In the new dispensation, 'the norms to which substantive rationality accords predominance include ethical imperatives, utilitarian and other expediential rules, and political maxims, all of which diverge from the formalism [of law] as well as from that which uses logical abstraction' (Weber, 1978, 894).

Jürgen Habermas' intervention on this point is helpful, as he deploys the distinction between 'law as medium' and 'law as institution' in *Theory of Communicative Action* to distinguish between the former instrumental and strategic uses of law, and the latter communicative and freedom-guaranteeing deployments. Juridification attaches to the former. Habermas explains that while 'juridification refers quite generally to the tendency towards an increase in formal law that can be observed in modern society', it is the qualitative distinction that matters between 'the expansion of law, that is the legal regulation of new, hitherto informally regulated social matters, from the increasing density of law, that is the specialized break-down of global statements of the legally relevant facts into more detailed statements' (1984, 357). Habermas argues that the process of juridification can generally be understood as part of a series of processes by which the modern state and the economy developed as distinctive bodies or systems that operate subject to their own distinctive rationalities (1984, pp. 530ff). So far this is akin to the way we have described differentiation. But for Habermas a pathology arises when a threshold is crossed, at which point these systemic logics begin to 'colonise' the field of their application. The term 'colonisation' here captures an unwarranted intrusion whereby the spheres of administration and the economy, which are directed to the instrumental demands to reproduce systems of power and money, impinge upon spontaneous societal practices – which Habermas designates by the term 'lifeworld'. The notion of *lifeworld* is borrowed from the phenomenological theories of Husserl, and then Gadamer, to capture the sense of the social embeddedness of practices, the quotidian experiences, attachments, and certainties of social life – in other words, the means that furnish belonging-ness and allow social actors to navigate their world. For Habermas, beyond a certain point this orientation-value is lost to the 'irresistible dynamic' of money and state power that operates according to an instrumental rational-ity. For this line of theorising, then, juridification is pitted against the spontaneous and self-determining aspects of the lifeworld where social actors experience their participation as meaningful. Juridification displaces these processes with a language and sets of standards that are not the participants'. The intrusion of the administrative logic of state power with its emphasis on social steering and control marks the displacement of lifeworld practices by rules that are pre-fixed,[23] heteronomous, precluding of alternatives, and therefore both 'patronising' (1984, 547) at the cost of dislocating the 'lifeworld' and depriving the citizens of the power of decision and self-determination.

It is worth dwelling a little longer on what is lost in the rise of the 'cognitive-instrumental' rationality that Habermas associates with the regulatory state, though the significance of this point also transfers directly to what we will say about 'politicisation' next. Key to the argument here is the assumption that the regulatory-welfare state was not able to *produce solidarities* but was only able to *compensate for their dissolution* under capitalism. This is a premise that is shared by theorists across the political spectrum, from the far left all the way to the *nouveaux philosophes* of the French 'new Right': citizens were not the active subjects of the regulatory state but its objects, recipients, clients, and so forth. In which case, 'social-statism', as Pierre Rosanvallon put it (2000), can only be understood as a *substitute* for society. Where for the left it created bonds of dependency to the capitalist state rather than solidarity, for the right, social-welfare regulation hampered economic initiative and entrepreneurial energies. These were discussions that dominated the latter decades of the previous century. Against the social-democratic commitment to the social state, an institution that after the war had made European societies able to function on a human scale, the New Right stormed the political landscape in the late 1970s with its vehement anti-collectivism, its disregard for solidarity, and its rampant defence of individualism. This is just for note; our own primary concern here is with the meaning of juridification in this context.

The analysis of the pathology that is 'juridification' might usefully bifurcate here. On the one hand, one may pursue it along a path that is *internal* to law and reflect on law's reflexivity, where the pathology concerns law's own integrity as a domain, field, or discourse. The second route concerns the *external* relation between law and the social fields that are subjected to juridification, what earlier we called 'performance'. Let us take them in turn.

In the first case, juridification names an unhelpful stretching of the institutional imagination of law that in the process surrenders something of the integrity of legal thought and the valued (always relative) fixity of its concepts, both key elements of the rule of law ideal. The rule of law firmly places law's sources in *past* decisions of bodies with jurisdictional power and looks for security and the stability of expectations in the sanction of law. Attempts to

---

[23] Indicatively Simitis with respect to labour relations: 'the juridification process confronts the employee with standardized patterns of behaviour, reshaping his lifeworld in accordance with the peculiar characteristics of these patterns and initiating increasingly internalized adaptation' (Simitis, 1987, 133).

introduce too much variety, responsiveness, malleability, and so forth in those categories gives up on that which is constitutive of law as the guarantor of order and expectations. The critiques of the 'materialisation' of law, of 'goal-oriented' legislation, of judicial discretion and judicial 'creativity', all express that unease. In each case, legal resources are extended to societal problems in ways that undermine law's constitutive features, and the result is experienced as juridification.

It is however in the second case, when the law is successful in exporting its rationality to the societal domain, that the external effects of that 'colonising' move (to return to Habermas' term) are most commonly felt and described as juridification. The interdependences that form and sustain the regulated fields (workplace, family, environment, etc.) are worked into law through legal self-descriptions of positions in law (employer–employee, spouses, seller–buyer, commissioner–commissioned, producer–consumer, etc.), in other words 'role systems'. Legal self-descriptions become more varied as law becomes more 'responsive' or 'material', but the variety is still produced by a proliferation of relevant positions that are *reductions*: relatively fixed points of allocation and address of subjectivity in law. Relations, cooperation, the multifarious forms of association, are couched in categories that preordain form and content, demarcate the problems, and pre-empt what can be said about them. Association is thus aligned to legal co-ordinates where concepts of rights, liberties, legal notions of harm and legal analogies, legal tests and legal presumptions first make sense of it. Who is entitled to associate or refrain from association, who can allege to have suffered harm or benefited, who counts as the disadvantaged party entitled to redress, why and when, as well as what enters the balance and what tilts the balance, to what side, all depend on a multitude of legal descriptions and conditional attributions that create the necessary relevancies and legal evaluations; in a word, all that is experienced as law. All these relevancies allow for social interdependence selectively. Juridification occurs beyond the threshold where law's classificatory operation – what we might call with Luhmann the 'redundancy' of legal thought – stifles and distorts, rather than expresses, the underlying polycentricity and variety of association.

Capturing both the above 'internal' and 'external' aspects, Teubner's early important discussion of juridification mapped it onto regulatory problems and quandaries. Taking his cue from the systems theoretical concept of 'structural coupling', Teubner spoke of the 'regulatory trilemma' that confronted the regulatory state as it attempted to navigate the coupling between the legal system, the political system, and the regulated field. There are, for Teubner, three ways in which the complex 'coupling' might become skewed and lead to regulatory failure; (1) where the law is deployed to regulate the field but fails to have any significant impact or 'steering', for example in cases of environmental protection where political initiatives remain ineffective, anaemic, or blunt; (2) where the logic of the regulated field overwhelms the regulating instance, for example in cases of 'market capture' where regulation *of* the market becomes captive *to* the market; and finally (3) where the regulated field is colonised by the logic of the regulating system and subjects itself to that alien rationality (Teubner, 1987, 21). It is this latter pathology that Teubner singles out as the case of 'juridification' par excellence.

Teubner's solution involves introducing and sustaining an element of reflexivity in the medium of law. His theory of 'reflexive law' counters the juridification effect visited on the regulated field by cultivating in the law an alertness and self-awareness of its limits. In this way is fashioned an intervention to ameliorate the effects and redistribute the costs of market allocations through the concept of 'reflexive' law – a *procedural* alternative to substantive intervention. Teubner pursues the explanation as a question of 'structural coupling' between the political system, where regulatory strategies are hammered out, the legal system, which is the former's means of implementing that policy, and the social field to be regulated, each with its own autonomous logic that defies direct manipulation. Problems of juridification then appear as overstepping boundaries and as failures to respect the distinctiveness of the systems involved on all sides in this delicate process of reflexive intervention.

These are complex discussions over the limits of intervention and regulation. We will have a chance to look at how questions of differentiation, of overstepping, of impinging and 'colonising' play out as complexity increases and modern society gradually submits to the exigencies of globalisation. But even before these developments, differentiation named a fragile, and contested, achievement. Contested because the *regulatory* uses of law, and the whole discussion of 'social engineering' (Roscoe Pound), tapped from the very beginning deeper societal conflicts over the legitimate use of public power and collective categories in the running of society and its economy. It is to these that we will turn next. Before we do, let us summarise the main argument about the asymmetry that we termed juridification. The *hypertrophy* of law, we argued, *internally* impacts on law's own ability to mobilise its own resources consistently; and *externally* is perhaps best understood in terms of institutional density that excessively reduces, distorts, or misses key aspects of the meaning that social actors attach to their practices. Historically, one of the most interesting theorisations was the denunciation of the 'petrification of labour relations', as the labour lawyers of the Weimar Republic put it, anxious that the political or class dimension of industrial conflict not be abated or lost to law's own rendering of the stakes and social forces involved in it. If Ernst Fraenkel put that in robust and explicit terms in Weimar, it was his contemporary and friend Otto Kahn-Freund who introduced the 'voluntary principle' in the context of industrial relations in the United Kingdom, with his insistence on 'collective laissez-faire' and on keeping the law out of the substantive regulation of labour relations, its role simply that of subtending (but not intruding in) their autonomous development.[24] Today the question over the juridification of labour relations has transferred largely over to the use of comparators, tests, and the 'open method of co-ordination' of national systems of labour protection, and so forth. In this vein, the exponents of soft law and light regulation warn that the law's function of securing expectations and the inertia that commits it to the past endanger both the dynamism and future orientation of market activity as well as of 'experimentalist' self-determination, beyond what is juridified as business-as-usual constitutional practice. Where under the aegis of functional differentiation, processes of coupling between economics, politics, and law are perceived to deploy these articulations productively, juridification instead names the threshold beyond which legal givens unduly *over*determine outcomes.

Politicisation

The concern that the political system not be allowed to override, to run unchecked, to elevate itself to a preferential position vis-à-vis all other societal rationalities, is familiar and endlessly renewed. The critique of politicisation comes predominantly in the form of two lines of argument. The first claims that where the exercise of political-constituent power remains unchecked, and where the collective power bestows upon itself the politicisation of all aspects of social life and the renegotiation of all that is fixed and entrenched in institutions, it leads to absolutism and terror. The Jacobin or the Bolshevik experience is typically recalled at this point. The second line ties politicisation to the hubris of assuming that a political society possesses the knowledge to steer itself, in the form of 'command economies' or the 'regulatory state'; here the critique comes with a professed modesty and the humility of a necessarily limited epistemology. This is a line of theorising associated with Hayek and renewed by Luhmann that argues that a functionally differentiated society is one that has no 'centre' remaining from which social demands can be articulated and directed

---

[24] Indicatively: 'The writer doubts whether the application of legal sanctions would be conducive to the better functioning of the existing organs of workers' representation and of joint consultation. ... the law can do very little to reinforce the willingness of both sides to co-operate. On the contrary the law's intervention may make rigid what ought to be flexible. ... In the writer's opinion it would be an illusion to think that the law can guarantee a functioning system of workers' representation ... the voluntary principle is sufficiently valuable to be purchase at the price of lack of realism in the law' (Kahn-Freund, 1954, 51).

to other systems. Familiar arguments against planning and command economies are typically rehearsed at this point. Our purpose here is to map, rather than dispel, these two lines of critique, and yet in both cases certain caveats must be inserted along the way.

Regarding the first line of critique, the revolutionary tradition bequeathed modern society with the constitutive hypothesis that democracy meant self-legislation, the exercise of the general will, and with it a mandate was granted to the political system to handle all societal thematics and demands through binding collective decision-making. While the exponential increase of the complexity of modern society has made such a democratic premise highly improbable (see Thornhill, 2018, ch. 1), its general rationale, however qualified, continues to inform a great deal of normative theory, including theories of discursive democracy by Habermas and others. But in those cases, the exercise of political power, however understood, is qualified, because it either articulates with the exercise of individual rights (as 'co-original' with democracy in Habermas, 1995) or is mediated through the exercise of constituted power. Outside these modes of mediation, the 'pure' expression of the political, when it breaks onto the scene of history as revolution and as democratic excess and its unmediated (by rights and controls) application, leads to terror. Such, goes the argument, is the risk of overt politicisation and the exercise of constituent power. In the standard formulation of the *fear of the political*, if constitutional-ism gives legal form to the political, it is so that 'the abysses and the temptations of the political are banned'.[25] The liberal theory of the public sphere, famously in the case of John Rawls, warns against the intrusion of political passions into public deliberative processes. 'For ... [some] ... the political relation may be that of friend or foe ... or it may be a relentless struggle to win the world for the whole truth. ... [But] the zeal to embody the whole truth in politics is incompatible with an idea of public reason that belongs with democratic citizenship'.[26] It is well known that Jacques Derrida also objected to constituent 'presence' and to theorising radical democracy as pure or immediate presentation, because, he argued, it inevitably involves the shading between radical democracy and totalitarianism.[27]

---

[25] Ulrich Preuss, quoted in Lindahl (2013, 210).

[26] Rawls (1997). See also van der Walt (2020).

[27] Derrida (1992). One might counter-suggest with Ernst Bloch: 'The fear of the demos, of the visible will that needs to be stabilized, turns dialectic into a movement in a closed house and leaves it standing still in the domain of law' (2018/1986, 125). Also Regis Debray: '*Totalitarianism* serves much the same function in the arsenal of our political science as fanaticism did in that of the Enlightenment or totemism in primitive anthropology: it is both an excuse for mis-recognition and a rite to ward off evil' (Debray, 1983, 11).

If such a 'prudential' argument against overt politicisation turns on the fear of the exercise of constituent power outwith the institutional guarantees of the constitutional framework, a second, more pervasive, and much proclaimed objection draws on epistemological grounds. The argument against assuming that complex modern societies can generate the kind of centralised knowledge that might allow their smooth and efficient 'steering' is typically associated with Friedrich von Hayek and his highly influential attack on social democracy and the welfare state. Hayek argued that the attempt at collective self-legislation through the political system and the political steering of the regulatory state in the direction of meeting social needs is highly inefficient, philosophically naive, and politically dangerous. Such politicisation, for Hayek, had been emphatically defeated in the discrediting of the 'command economies' of the Soviet bloc that propped up the inefficiencies of the political steering of the economic system with state terror. A long line of theorists of the New Right have rehearsed these arguments, sometimes renewing or radicalising them in a neoliberal direction, arguing for a shrinkage of the political system and the expansion of market thinking. In a profoundly Hayekian vein, Luhmann too railed against what he called 'goal-oriented programming' in law (Luhmann, 1990a), which denoted the uses of law that were harnessed to the achievement of political goals as opposed to the rule-of-law-like protection of expectations of the type that Hayek had designated as *catallaxy*: the legal regime of property and rights that comprise the institutional structure of support for his 'free society'. We will need to look at 'marketisation' before we can fully appreciate the novelty of this epistemological displacement. But, in any case, it is in terms of political steering, 'social engineering', and the rise of the regulatory-welfare state that the hypertrophy of the political system has been most vehemently criticised in the notion of 'politicisation'. The welfare state emerged after World War II as a pervasive self-description of the political system, arrogating to itself the resolution of social problems that, crucially for its critics, originated in *other* function systems. The way in which politics were universalised in this way, presenting all social problems as problems that could be solved politically, is for Luhmann, as it is for Hayek, a disquieting assumption. On the one hand, as Luhmann would insist throughout his analysis of the political system, the 're-entry' of complex unsolvable problems into the political system as politically solvable problems allowed welfare states to secure their own autopoiesis. But of course the operative autonomy of function systems – what we have been describing as functional differentiation – makes problematic such crossings. That is not to say that they are not productive to the political system. It is not even to say that all – or most – steering will be unsuccessful. It is to say that whether it is successful or not is something that the political system will decide for itself, and whether the solutions were or were not successful becomes impossible to say. Such is the crucial knowledge deficit that Luhmann points to. And it is a deficit that maps directly onto functional differentiation as the condition for the development of a complex society, against the hierarchisation, expansion, and predominance of the political system of the regulatory state and the necessary reductions it carries, that are felt on the register of differentiation and, in the way Luhmann has laid the cards, also therefore as obstacles to individual inclusion and freedom (see above on 'the role of human rights'). For him, under conditions of complexity, the necessarily partial rationality of the political system cannot and should not be elevated to any kind of primacy, and both socialist states and welfare-regulatory states (significantly, with respect to the role they assume, Luhmann does not differentiate between the two) threaten the very fabric of society with de-differentiation, if the claims of the political system are inflated and the role of the state seen as the 'shaping of society' (Luhmann, 1990a, and Thornhill, 2018, 125).

More than in the case of the other 'asymmetries' we are looking at, the question over what is *adequate* differentiation, and what it means to keep the *political* system from excessive intrusion, is unquestionably normative and highly politicised. As already suggested, the critique of the 'intrusion' was key to the successful rhetoric of the New Right (in both the United States and the United Kingdom in the 1970s) with the alleged 'exhaustion' of the regulatory-welfare state. Whatever response we give to the future of the particular organisational form, the ability of a society politically to control social production, participation, and distribution remains of the essence and determines how the asymmetry of politicisation is read, what the measure of 'excessive intrusion' (of politics into 'the economy') is, and what it means for the balance to be restored. And it is the same question of proper measure that allows us to navigate the final of the asymmetries next, this time as it relates to the hypertrophy of the market.

Marketisation

The most pronounced and currently unassailable form of asymmetry that cuts away at differentiation relates to *the hypertrophy of the economic system*. The ascendancy of economic reason today is of staggering significance.

Michel Foucault, who gave us one of the most careful accounts of this genealogy, describes the 'birth of biopolitics' in terms of the recalibration of the operations that we have called *performance*, that is, in terms of a renewal of the coupling of the political, legal, and economic systems. He describes the shift, how the 'raison d' Etat' in the late eighteenth century reoriented itself from the political to the economic system, in a way that allowed it to determine its proper scope, consolidate its semantics, and receive its internal self-limitation. What, asks Foucault, was the 'internal instrument, the form of calculation and rationality that made possible the self-limitation of governmental reason?' And he answers: 'Obviously it is political economy' (2004, 13).

Now, while what is 'political' about this 'political economy' remains something of a blind spot in Foucault's account, the emergence during the late eighteenth century in Europe of what Karl Polanyi identified as the 'market *system*'[28] enabled the following extraordinary evolutionary achievement in terms of the coupling of politics, law, and the economy. For state law, the emergence of the market system plays the role of catalyst as it confronted it with the 'truth' of natural equilibria. Against this 'truth' governmental action could measure the legitimacy of its reach and intervention. The rationale of *self-limitation* thus acquired an external measure, with the help of which a role proper for public law was fashioned. From that point on a coupling with the economic system would ensure the proper self-limitation of political power, and the principle that 'one must not govern too much' was granted a means to rationalise what that 'excess' meant. It was therefore no longer about an *internal* measure, in the way in which Machiavelli had envisaged the reflexive reference of the exercise of political power. Instead, the new development marked a move away from the logic of 'sovereignty' and the transcendence of that entire paradigm. Foucault traces the historical trajectory of that transcendence (2000): in the premodern period, he writes, governance proceeds in conformity with moral, natural, and divine laws; in the sixteenth and seventeenth centuries it is identified with raison d'état and driven by Machiavelli's question: 'Am I governing with sufficient intensity so as to bring the State to its maximum strength?' Now, with the shift to the political economy, the logic of rule acquires an *external* reference and with it a new measure: *am I governing too much or too little given 'the nature of things'*? With this latter shift is borne the governmental regime called 'liberalism', says Foucault. The orientation of public law in terms of the guiding distinction of public/private delimits proper spheres of application and a rationale for intervention, and the economy becomes equipped with the sets of concepts that will both enable and structure market activity. The identification of what is 'proper' thereby also informs legitimacy, connecting it to the *veridiction* of the market and what is now being launched as the *natural* truth of the spontaneous order. 'Political economy reflects on governmental practices, and it does not question them to determine whether or not they are

---

[28] Polanyi (1944). Foucault places the emergence of the 'political economy' between 1750 and 1830.

legitimate in terms of right. It considers them in terms of their effects rather than their origins', he writes (2004, 15). It in turn bestows a certain *naturalness* to the practice of governance. The role of the 'natural' – in this crucial sense of *human nature* – subtends the operation of governmentality, providing it with a rationale for actions and limits, in other words its *measure*. To govern correctly is to take on board the nature of the governed subject, to reflect the natural predicament of man, or, when it comes to forms of collective action, to reflect the natural results of co-ordinated activity between individual actions, a co-ordination that is expressed as market equilibria, that are just, not because they provide just outcomes, but because they are reflective, without distortion, of natural preferences. To 'govern too much' thereafter sees the 'excess' judged not on older criteria of reasonable exercise of 'raison d'état' but simply as missing or misrepresenting natural equilibria.

Clearly there is *nothing 'natural'* about this vision of human nature if one probes deeper, as Polanyi wonderfully reminds us when he writes with respect to Adam Smith's account of the rationality of the *homo oeconomicus* that never had such a *misreading* of human *nature* been so prophetic, in terms of the development of the market system (Polanyi, 1944). Notwithstanding this essential *misspelling* – this violation of the grammar of human interaction – for the physiocrats, as for Adam Smith, the freedom of the market can and must function in such a way that what they call *the natural price* be established through, and thanks to, market freedom. Add to this the 'natural sanction' of hunger with Malthus,[29] and nothing short of the human condition itself comes to sanction the market mechanism for the distribution of resources and the measure of the value of things. The idea of the 'natural' price comes to displace the notion of a 'just' price, of the kind that had structured market activity in the sixteenth and seventeenth centuries and expressed the complex of relationships involving the needs of the merchants, the quantity and quality of the work performed, the consumers' needs and possibilities, and so forth. '"Just price" was that which would neither disgust merchants nor wound consumers. But by the 1750s, the shift to natural or spontaneous mechanisms was underway. 'Natural price' rather than 'just price' became that which 'adequately express[ed] the relationship, a definite adequate relationship between the cost of production and the extent of demand', and 'no longer had any connotations of justice' (Foucault, 2004, 31). 'Inasmuch as prices are determined in accordance with

---

[29] Malthus had famously argued that the 'sanction of hunger' lay at the root of the law governing the growth of population, and in the labour market played the decisive role in the determination of wages. Population is limited by the means of subsistence at its disposal. Any interference – through private or public charity – with the food supply threw the whole system off balance (Malthus, 1992/1798).

the natural mechanisms of the market they constitute a standard of truth which enables us to discern which governmental practices are correct and which are erroneous'. Therefore, 'inasmuch as it enables production, need, supply, demand, value and price to be linked together through exchange, the market constitutes a site of veridiction' (32). Veridiction brings the question of justice to face up to the truth of natural equilibria, and political rationality encounters its limit at what is devoid of alternatives.

But, of course, highly questionable assumptions support the generalisation of market thinking and the kind of 'governmental naturalism' that Foucault speaks about as emerging at this time around 'the internal and intrinsic mechanics of economic processes' to be *discovered* and to be known by government, in their 'innermost and complex nature' (Foucault, 2004, 61). The emergence of these certitudes is certainly a pressing matter for the rising class of industrialists 'anxious', as Eric Roll puts it in the *History of Economic Thought*, 'to sweep away all restrictions on the market and on the supply of labor – the remnants of the out-of-date regime of merchant capital and the landed interest' (Roll, 1956, 156). These were 'certitudes' that were 'discovered', and it was 'laws' that buttressed such discoveries. One of the most important discoveries of such 'laws' was that articulated by Jean-Baptiste Say as the 'law of markets' in his *Traité d' Economie Politique*, published in Paris on the heels of Adam Smith's *Wealth of Nations*, which came to serve as a foundation of the classical and neoclassical doctrine in economics.[30] In Kenneth Galbraith's formulation of it, 'it asserts that the economy finds its equilibrium at full employment, and from full employment comes the flow of demand that sustains it' (Galbraith, 1987, 221). 'Say's law' tells us that the economy reaches *natural* equilibria, that production creates its own demand, and that periodic crises – during which goods go unsold and labour power goes without employment – are simply part of law-like business cycles where dislocations are temporary opportunities for the economy to readjust at the optimal level. The resilience of this 'law' can only be appreciated by the resilience of the classical and neoclassical models that it sustains. Even as late as 1933, even after the Great Depression had wrought havoc, and with unemployment in the USA still at around 25 per cent of the labour force, no less influential a figure as Arthur Pigou at Cambridge would write: '[w]ith perfectly free competition there will always be a strong tendency towards full employment. Such unemployment as exists at any time is due wholly to the frictional resistances that prevent the appropriate wage and price adjustments being made instantaneously'.[31] It is only under the later influence of Keynes that the realisation came, and was accepted,

---

[30] Still referred to in economics textbooks as 'Say's law'. See Galbraith (1987).

[31] Pigou, *The Theory of Unemployment,* quoted in Galbraith (1987, 212).

that natural equilibria were ordinarily struck at suboptimal levels (the 'under-employment equilibrium'). And it was with Keynes that the 'naturalness' of the market assumptions was (however temporarily) shaken, and the management of aggregate demand became a political question, that is, a question of state management of the economy. But that was much later.

Let us stay with this question: what are the elements that lead to the hypertrophy that is 'marketisation'? We might identify two steps in the way that the elevation of *economic truth* is placed above and as determining of other systemic rationalities. As a limit to *political* governance, and as a measure of law's performance, the new prominence of the market destroys the heterarchy that was functional differentiation.[32] And, while marketisation occurs at the interface between the economic and political systems, providing the signs that enable the structures, mechanisms, and justifications of power to function and offering the coupling through which politics establishes its particular rationality, the *dissymmetry* between the two systems lies in this: that no reciprocity or equivalence governs the relationship. As a condition of unfolding of the new rationality, the '*political* economy' is overdetermined by one side of the coupling, and no equivalent contribution is offered in the other direction, *from* politics *to* the economy. Foucault calls this the 'dissymmetrical bipolarity of politics and the economy' (2004, 20). Already for us, and for our concern with differentiation, balance, and 'performance', something important has occurred in terms of the elevation of the economic criterion *above* other function systems.

But there is a second step, beyond the 'dissymmetry', where economic reason does not merely displace other rationalities *but substitutes for them*. 'If', Foucault reminds us, 'there is an inverse circuit going from the state to the economic constitution, it should not be forgotten that the element that comes first in this kind of siphon is the economic constitution. There is a permanent genesis, a permanent genealogy of the state from the economic constitution'. And he continues:

> This economic institution, the economic freedom that from the start it is the role of this institution to guarantee and maintain, produces something even more real, concrete and immediate than a legal legitimation; it produces a permanent consensus of all those who may appear as agents within these economic processes, as investors, workers, employers and trade unions. All these economic partners produce a consensus, inasmuch as they accept this economic game of freedom. (Foucault, 2004, 84)

---

[32] Gorz summarises it well when he writes that 'economic rationality was, for a long time held in check not only by tradition, but also by other types of rationality ... which set the limits that were not to be exceeded. Industrial capitalism was only able to take off when economic rationality freed itself from all the other principles of rationality and submitted them to its dictatorial control' (Gorz, 1989, 18–19).

In this notion of the 'permanent consensus', something significant has occurred. The consensus concerns the terms that the 'economic constitution' imports to the exclusion of any alternatives at the level of posing the question. The market's *move to the metalevel*, where it sets the terms of possible agreement and disagreement, completes and seals its elevation.[33] Its promise to unlock the hierarchical logic of (state) organisation, to counter the logic of command, and to release societal energies down heterarchical routes and trajectories sets forth an irrepressible dynamic. If the privileging of its own criteria for what counts as rational is occluded in the move that elevates the price mechanism into criterion of veridiction, and thereby generalises economic reason, it is no less a decisive move of de-differentiation for that. Marketisation, like juridification and politicisation before it, names a pathology, a hypertrophy of a single system at the expense of others; it names functional overreach.

Conclusion

Differentiation is a precarious achievement. And if that precarity is glaringly obvious in the sweeping popularity of the reductionisms that contest it, notably the 'law and economics' varieties, it is evident even in the work of its 'champions'. Already in 1990 Luhmann would add a word of caution that constitutionalism had transcended the 'evolutionary achievement' that was the national-constitutional order. As politics are endlessly confronted with problems that can no longer be referred to questions of sovereignty, he says, and as law is no longer predominantly about the regulation of conflict but increasingly geared to the production and programming of specific outcomes, 'perhaps', he suggests, 'we are deceived in our fascination for the Constitution and the acknowledgement of its value, ... about how far advanced we are on a path that has long left behind these foundations' (1990, 215).

This poses the question that we will explore in the next and final section of this Element. While there is nothing *compelling* – in the sense of either necessary or incontrovertible – about the underlying assumptions of Luhmann's diagnosis,[34] the emphasis he puts on the constitution and its changing significance returns us to a key point of our analysis. The role of the constitution,

---

[33] For this argument, see Christodoulidis (2021).

[34] If the autonomy and differentiation of law matters as a conceptual issue, its significance must be sought at a deeper level from these projects and projections: that of Hayek's of installing highly contingent and conjectural political preferences as generalisable conditions of correct theory; and of Luhmann's of appending his call against 'de-differentiation' to an argument about functional adequacy supposedly shorn of any normative grounding. These are substantive political arguments that have hoisted themselves to the metalevel on the back of highly questionable assumptions.

which is to orchestrate the difficult balance and sustain the articulation between society's key functional systems – law, politics, and the economy – depends on its own reflexive control of the legal system's unity. The constitution sets up the conditions of the interface between law and politics, and between law and the economy, and at the same time it manages the interface between the semantics of law and material practices (work, etc.). How to sustain and mobilise differentiation in this context is a profoundly difficult task for the legal system, which must confront the challenge of sustaining its own rationality, the *ratio juris*, from co-option, subjection, colonisation, and so forth, to and by other rationalities. With our attention on the differentiation and the autonomy of law, what does it mean to return law to its own proper insight and intelligence, its distinctiveness and dignity, which involves its proper articulation with, but not subsumption to, political power or economic efficiency? What does it mean, in other words, to sustain it at a critical distance from, and critical engagement with, both the competing rationalities and the material practices of the society whose legal system it is? This critical move must negotiate on the one side the distinctiveness of law's proper semantic resources, the concepts and integrity of legal reason, and on the other the relation of those semantics to the structures and processes that reproduce society at the level of its material practices.

An important recent restatement of the integrity of the *ratio juris* is Alain Supiot's *Homo Juridicus*. For Supiot, the achievement of juridical reason is to provide the shared symbolic medium that *binds* by 'interposing shared meaning between people' (2007, xxiv). What the law achieves, across societies and history, is to generate forms of this bond, and by means of which also, a reciprocity that rests on obligations assumed. 'Binding' and 'interposing', reciprocity and obligation: words that, for Supiot, sustain at the foundational level the meaning of 'the human' and of 'the common' *in tandem*. In mining a deep hermeneutics, Supiot offers us a radical recuperation of juridical reason, where the juridical is recovered as distinct from, and as irreducible to, various reductionisms, crucially that of law to economic reason.

If the return to the notion of systemic autonomy and of the differentiation of logics or spheres of action appears as a minority theoretical position in the sweeping methodological turn to the economy today, it is no less significant, or urgent, for that. The suggestion pursued here is that its importance be scrutinised from a methodological point of view that does not already surrender law's perspective to the prevalence of economic reason. Key to this is the deployment of critical theory, in the sense of one both oriented to practice and self-consciously normative. The idea is that the levels of analysis (conceptual, systemic, institutional) lend important and non-cumulative perspectives, and they orient research away from the usual ways of looking at these questions and the unhelpful categories that structure current debate in a way that simply reproduces the problematic assumptions that frame it. Instead, the autonomous and differentiated legal system navigates a distinctive course between its own formalism and its relation to society.

Let it be said again that the diagnoses of what is a 'proper' boundary, what an adequate 'performance', what an 'asymmetry', what 'functional' against what 'oversteps', are all questions with heavy normative import. Because, of course, as it has already become clear, a larger discussion is staked on differentiation. If there is a danger of overstepping the 'boundaries' that carve up the functionally differentiated domain of society, it is because the resultant pathologies mark a diminishment of capacity to act in the relevant field and to protect the values that pertain to it. The diminishment of capacity entails also costs in terms of inclusion of diverse actors and their experience of the loss of meaning. At the same time, the allocation of distinct thematics to differentiated spheres, the distributions of what is rational as proper to distinct logics of action, severs connections that are themselves constitutive of claiming, or claiming-back, stakes of democratic participation, association, and decision-making in the political economy from the logic of price. Critical thinking is vital at these junctures, and before these antinomies and dilemmas. In any case, questions heavy with normative resonance attach to these balances and their proper maintenance, and this is the case in particular under the pressures of globalisation and the pressure to increase the rates of return for global capital. It is to this that we will now turn.

3 The Autonomy of Law and the Challenge of Globalisation

Global Functional Differentiation

Functional differentiation, Luhmann once joked, is like the original sin: it cannot be undone, and no return to the original condition is possible. The levity of the reference belies how profoundly functional differentiation separates and entrenches logics of action and 'spheres of justice', in a way that sets the logic of the accumulation of capital on its tracks, subjecting it to economic rules of motion. Is it a coincidence, we might then ask, that Marx had famously drawn the same reference to original sin in his discussion of original, or primitive, accumulation? 'Adam bit the apple, and thereupon sin fell on the human race'.[35]

---

[35] The relevant section from *Capital* I (ch. 26, 'The secret of primitive accumulation') reads: 'This primitive accumulation plays in Political Economy about the same part as original sin in theology. Adam bit the apple, and thereupon sin fell on the human race'.

As we were able to trace in Section 1, the rise of modernity came with a shift away from stratification and towards a differentiation of functional domains. The differentiation has to do with the gradual autonomisation of spheres and logics of social action and the development of separate semantics for the differentiated fields. Primitive accumulation was the original act of dispossession that destroyed the forms of the social bond and of social production under feudalism and ushered in the autonomous forms, fields, and logics of action that heralded the age of capital. Now society came to appear as the sum of heterarchically positioned partial rationalities and as 'multi-rational' in the sense that no single set of values or norms could be perceived as universally applicable: no trans-systemic rationality could claim to be the source of values or norms, and no overarching value system should compromise inner-systemic rationalisation. We looked at all of this earlier, and we looked at the meaning of differentiation and the principle of linkage that supported functional interdependence. As far as the legal system is concerned, the constitution had a special role to play in securing the autonomy and differentiation of law. The interface between the subsystems – of law, politics, the economy – involved a series of articulations (that took the form of 'structural coupling') that were harboured in, and enabled by, the constitution, under the purview of the nation-state. Significantly, the careful architecture of functional rationalities was from the start of the project of modernity super-coded to capitalist conditions, operations, and distributions. One can trace the articulations along all of the inter-systemic borders, in terms of what we earlier called 'performance': the legal system's 'performance' vis-à-vis the political system is that it channels the exercise of political power, provides rules for the exercise of government and state administration, sets the limits in terms of rights, and so forth; its performance vis-à-vis the economic system is to provide for the institutionalisation of economic relations (through property title and freedom of contract principally), to attribute liability and responsibility to economic actors (e.g. corporations), to regulate economic competition through competition law, and so forth. It is here, and in terms of performance, that the law sets the autopoiesis of the self-regulating capitalist economic system on its tracks.

An important caveat needs to be inserted at this point. While functional differentiation ensured the smooth running of the economy on its own values (eigenvalues) and modalities in the advanced capitalist economies of the *metropolitan* centres of commerce and industry, the *colonies* enjoyed none of the 'self-limitation' of the political and the legal systems, which were instead exported to secure 'exploitation by dispossession'.[36] Even where the extraction

---

[36] On the meaning of exploitation by dispossession see in particular Harvey (2003).

of surplus value from the colony was primarily channelled through economic institutions that typically took the form of licensed corporations (e.g. the East India Company), it was buttressed by devastating operations of dispossession and suppression in the violent, extractive colonial economy. In that sense, *empire*, rather than the nation-state, is capitalism's typical territorial form.[37] As we move to discuss globalisation, some of the lineages feature stark. If, under globalisation, the relation between the metropolis and the periphery is no longer structured along imperial lines, the extraction of surplus value takes new, diverse, usually less overt forms.

That is at least one way to approach globalisation, through the perspective of empire. Definitions of globalisation, of course, abound. In all cases globalisation can be relatively uncontroversially understood as referring to the operation of the economy at the supranational level, an operation poised to ensure that the global flows of capital maximise its rates of return by circumventing the loci of labour and social protection. When it comes to law, the advent of globalisation has a radical effect on the capacity of the law to perform its function as we have described it, and to secure its 'performance' vis-à-vis the economy. At the level of the political and legal systems, globalisation has forced a comprehensive shift where, once uploaded to the transnational level, constitutional processes appear to be beyond the purview of political control, because politics are still very much conducted at national level, in terms of what is enacted as democratic law. As a result, what traditionally inspired the thinking of democratic self-legislation now finds most of the matters of distribution and justice are beyond its reach, dictated by activity conducted at the supranational level. 'Global law', no longer defined through 'pedigree' or origin in democratic enactment, is the name of what transfers upward – from the statal to the supra-statal – as the means of regulation of that activity.

First let us see how the emergence of 'global law', whatever its precise features, affects our discussion of its autonomy, and whether law's differentiation as a system does not constitute one of the first casualties of its upscaling to the planetary level.

Gunther Teubner provides a good entry point into this set of concerns: 'Globalization above all', he says, 'means that functional differentiation, first realised historically within the nation states of Europe and North America, now encompasses the whole world. Certainly not all subsystems have globalized simultaneously, with the same speed and intensity. Religion, science and the economy are well established as global systems, while politics and law still remain mainly focused on the nation state' (Teubner, 2012, 42). 'The staggered

---

[37] For this argument see Savage (2021).

nature of globalisation produces a tension between the self-foundation of autonomous global social systems and their political-legal constitutionalisation' (43). Teubner raises the question of this 'tension' to point out that the 'constellation' that was possible in the nation-state between law, politics, and the regulated field (subsystem) has come undone; that there is 'no counterpart' to it 'in the global context'; and that 'global self-foundation and national constitutionalisation are irrevocably drifting apart' (44). The discrepancy between 'globally established social subsystems and a politics stuck at inter-state level' can only lead to 'the constitutional totality break[ing] apart' to be 'replaced by a form of constitutional fragmentation' (51). As a result, '[t]he comprehensive structural coupling' that Luhmann famously identified as an 'evolutionary achievement' in the constitution of nation-states in modernity clearly has no equivalent at the level of world society' (52). We have instead a 'new phenomenon: the self-constitutionalization of global orders without a state' (53), which is the basis of Teubner's theory of world 'societal constitutionalism'. We will return to 'societal constitutionalism' as one of the proffered solutions, later, but for now let it be noted that for Teubner this development is not without its benefits. His assumption is that with the new societal form of 'self-constitutionalisation of global orders', the constitutional *function* might be uploaded from national to global level, where function – as definitive of what it is to have a constitution – is less marked by a dependency on 'the power of states, state policies and the ideologies of political parties'.

We might suggest that the problem that globalisation poses for the legal system is that it leaves it in *a split condition. On the one side* of the split, at the level of the national state, the law is left with limited functions: in the mode of facilitating the 'experimentalist' regulation of 'soft' instruments, benchmarks, incentives, 'regulatory sandboxes', and the whole ludic panoply of soft law that comes with globalisation and complements the very 'hard' and punitive clamp-down on syndicalist freedoms and industrial action that it requires of the nation-state. Typically, then, as economic decision-making moves upward to supranational levels, national law is left largely to provide policing and enforcement and, significantly, to ensure 'preparedness for the market'.[38] The role of the state in the implementation of structural adjustment programmes in the developing world, and of 'conditionalities' in Europe's 'periphery' in the age of austerity, provides devastating evidence of this. Constitutional ideals have *migrated* (in Choudry's (2007) memorable formulation) to the transnational level, either

---

[38] This is not to suggest that the national legal systems have been weakened as sources of normative obligation. On the contrary, it has been argued that national and transnational law develop in a complementary way that mutually intensifies their impact. On *not* conceiving of the national-transnational relation in zero-sum terms see Kjaer (2014).

regional or global, as have key functions where the regulation of global production is concerned. *On the other side of the split*, at the global level, the postnational legal landscape regenerates the complexity that law's function (at a national level) had been understood to reduce, by virtue of its sheer range and diversity. And, as Neil Walker puts it in his important *Intimations of Global Law*, also by its 'fluidity of form, its multiplication of new forms of legally coded identity and difference, its congestion, its cross-systemic overlapping claims and focal concerns, its mechanisms of mutual recognition and deadlock; and it follows, its irreducibility to a state-sovereignist logic of mutually exclusive jurisdictional allocation' (2014, 56). The question of what remains of law as an institutional 'reduction-achievement', as systems theory invited us to understand it, is one that it becomes increasingly difficult to ask today, as it is difficult to identify what threshold holds law back from dissipating into management. We will confront this question as we move to discuss the 'challenges' and the proffered 'solutions'.

'Global' functional differentiation is poised on the breach. In the light of the aspiration to upload functional differentiation to the global scale, and to secure the role of an autonomous and differentiated system of 'global law', key problems arise. Functional differentiation depends on, and reproduces, a careful architecture of mutual performances; and if the new rationalities of the economy, of politics, of the range of differentiated spheres, remain meaningful in this precarious new global dispensation, it is for the demands they place on the reflexion of systems in terms of self-limitation and the maintenance of proper boundaries. But how difficult it now becomes to *ground* this reflexion in the shifting sands of globalisation.

Functional differentiation, once 'uploaded' to the global level, surrenders its achievements and generates an asymmetry that, having achieved an initial incursion in a system, proliferates under its own momentum. This is what we experience as the *generalisation of economic reason*.[39] The 'absolutising' of one systemic rationality – the economic – once elevated above those of the political and legal systems instrumentalises them and in the process magnifies the inequality that functional differentiation had promised to preclude. What is problematic about uploading its familiar pattern of 'coupling' and adjustment from the national to the supranational level is that it ignores the asymmetry between the economy and the legal–political complex, in other words between the transnationalisation of markets and that of states. The point is that the asymmetry is not a temporary or redressable anomaly; it is instead *structurally* built into *the architecture of global capitalism*. In the case of Europe, the asymmetry shows in the unevenness of the integration of national markets (through the fast-tracking of economic integration)

---

[39] For this concept see Gorz's excellent book of 1983.

as against the fragmentation of states' systems of social protection. At the level of 'world society', it is seen in the hugely successful creation of 'global turbo-capitalism' against the multi-fragmented processes of political transnationalisation. In each case the asymmetry is vital and productive for the integration of capital and the extraction of profit. The idea that a transnational system, *whose very logic of connectivity* (the 'trans' of the transnational) *plays out that of competition* (amongst national systems) and comparative advantage, might nevertheless act to rein in what sustains it is paradoxical. We are depressingly familiar with the ways in which the transnational is organised along the lines of managing 'preparedness for the market' –through the 'un-protecting' of labour, the suppression of wages and undercutting of trade unionism, the rolling back of the main costs of labour reproduction back onto labour, the abiding by World Bank governance manuals and the rest. The relation between capitals and states is crucial here, and the asymmetry propels the creation of margins of profit in terms of the 'race to the bottom', where social protection afforded by states are 'costs', and where any attempt to hoist it – social protection, that is – above the national to the European level (EU social chapter, social charter, social rights, social dialogue) is systematically undercut. Relations of core and peripheral states is a vital part of the 'rationalisation' and structure of the transnational. Spectacularly here, more than any other sphere of legal thinking, the reflexivity of the legal and political systems is short-circuited back into the market paradigm.

In all this, *functionality* (as principle of differentiation and as answer to complexity) walks a fine line. On the register of *differentiation*, where the division of labour names an interdependence, the maintenance of order must avoid the risk that interdependence splinters into fragmentation, which is precisely what globalisation threatens. On the register of *inclusion* where, as the proponents of differentiation would have it (human rights) law delivers the dividends of a flourishing, multifaceted agency, what is risked is exclusion and the withdrawal of recognition. And on the register of *normativity*, the ability of a political society to employ law to organise its *self*-legislation and *self*-determination appears to dissipate. We will discuss these various challenges under the headings of 'fragmentation', 'inclusion', and 'normativity'; and in a tentative vein finish by outlining suggested solutions.

The Nature of the Challenge

The Problem of Fragmentation

To put it in a nutshell, the question of justice is vulnerable to scaling up because such scaling up – from national to global – threatens to collapse differentiation into fragmentation. It is crucial to see and to insist on the difference between differentiation and fragmentation. Differentiation names *a principle of connection* that holds the parts together meaningfully – as differentiated and therefore as maintaining a relationship both to the whole and amongst themselves. Fragmentation, on the other hand, simply means *scattering*; it marks the move away from the whole to brokenness.

Let us be reminded that the 'constitutional achievement' is premised on reflexion, which is what undergirds and sustains the unity of the system. This implies that in the hierarchical system that is the constitution, certain values, typically democratically decided, are entrenched and held onto at higher levels, and inform the rationalisation of the law at lower levels. Globalisation erodes unity and therefore constitutional reflexion as based on entrenchment, hierarchisation, and rationalisation. At the level of the national constitution, the concepts of sovereign democratic enactment and control have been given over to a significant extent to non-statal bodies. This is well known, endlessly rehearsed and commented on.[40] But at the global level, too, however ample the accommodations of global law, however 'divergent' we are prepared to accept that it is, a certain threshold of unity *has to* be maintained for the law to be identified as such, in other words for the signifier 'law' to designate a reference and not to become 'empty'.[41] And it is under the constitutive notion of unity that law's organising concepts and distinctions perform the hard work of tracking the tolerable level of variation that allows us to collect disparate elements into its ambit. Luhmann reminds us that there will forever be centrifugal forces undermining law's unity, and globalisation certainly confronts the law with those centrifugal tendencies. Yet, against this move of differentiation, understood as the pull of divergent and overlapping jurisdictions, there is a force of 'redundancy' at play, Luhmann argues, one that sets a threshold of 'tolerable' – for the system – variation. The unity of the law then depends on this gathering of incongruous elements around its existing categories and descriptions, which are re-embedded as the legal system goes on. The system only continues – and in our case the system of global law only emerges *as a system* – if the disciplining effect works, if the balance between redundancy and variety is maintained as productive for it. In all this, and marking the moment of unity, is a certain 'gathering' rationalisation around organising principles. The unity of the system is strengthened through redundancy, which allows the activation of known grounds in every expansion onto new terrain, and conversely the institutional imagination comes undone if variety tips the system beyond the threshold where unity collects it. Then, the fragmented system of *global law* becomes the

---

[40] See Dobner and Loughlin (2010) for a landmark publication.
[41] On empty signifiers see Laclau (1996) and Christodoulidis (2020).

contested signifier *of random selections*, floated across fields of equivalence where it names everything and nothing at all, available to sanction any conceivable consolidation of interest, as long as the interests are powerful enough.

The test of 'proportionality' as exercised by the Court of Justice of the European Union (CJEU) as 'constitutional method' par excellence is a clear instance of the erosion of unity and of constitutional 'fragmentation' as we have been describing it. In the notorious 'quartet' of cases that came to be referred to as its 'Laval/Viking jurisprudence',[42] the CJEU decided on grounds of proportionality that where there had been a clash between national-constitutional labour protection and economic freedoms, national labour protection guarantees would have to cede as placing disproportionate limits on transnational economic freedoms. The judges determined that 'while the right to take collective action for the protection of the workers of the host state against possible social dumping may constitute an overriding reason of public interest . . . which, in principle, justifies a restriction of one of the fundamental freedoms guaranteed by the Treaty', the unions' exercise of the fundamental right to strike in pursuit of 'the legitimate public interest objective of worker protection' needed to be *proportionate*.[43] Crucial to this test, for our analysis, is that it is the circulation of 'social protection' and the 'dignity of labour' as two amongst many constitutional goods, including 'freedom of movement' (of capital and services), that sustains the reasoning and the decision. The dignity of labour is circulated *alongside* and *on par with* other constitutional goods like property rights and economic freedoms, and that the constitutional decision is about balancing them against each other. The 'social' constitution is released alongside the 'economic' constitution, and the constitutional goods they each sanction and protect circulate as other commodities, with the co-ordinates of their competition undone from any overall framework. Because to have 'circulation' *at all*, what is required is a principle of circulation and a common measure.[44] The proliferation of constitutions and the collapse of their internal hierarchisations, as well as any hierarchisation amongst them, contribute to the *undistorted* circulation of constitutional goods as commodities. Preference, unmoored from any of these constitutions or any value system, becomes the principle of choice. It becomes, in other words, a selection without constitutional warranty that substitutes constitutionality for outcome optimisation, which is a market

---

[42] Case C-341/05, *Laval un Partneri Ltd*, ECR 2007, I-11767; Case C-438/05, *International Transport Workers' Federation and Finnish Seamen's Union v Viking Line ABP and OÜ Viking Line Eesti*, ECR 2007, I-10779; Case C–446/06, *Rüffert v. Land Niedersachsen* [2008] ECR I–1167; 4 Case C–319/06, *Commission v. Luxembourg* [2009] ECR I–4323.

[43] Viking *ITWF v Viking Line*, Para 103.

[44] In Christodoulidis (2021) I suggested that at this point a default *market* constitutionalism installs itself.

principle, not a constitutional one. And while most labour lawyers have been critical of the decisions of the CJEU, they have done so very little to allay the fears that the price of European integration involves precisely this form of distribution of the risks of production that is referred to as 'social dumping';[45] and this of course is a distribution that does not, and cannot, receive constitutional warrant, except a posteriori and in the context of a fragmented constitutional order.

A great deal more can, and has, been said about the 'market turn' in global law. And, of course, the assessment of what political publics on the global scale might achieve cannot and should not be underestimated: global economic action inevitably generates global constituencies of addressees and therefore also global challenges. Teubner writes, for example, that 'the dismantling of national barriers and an explicit policy of deregulation led to a ... global financial market constitution that set free uncontrolled dynamics. ... Only with the near catastrophe we have experienced does it appear that collective learning processes will in future seek constitutional limitations' (2011b, 11). This is important, but it leaves us with the question: if 'learning processes' are indeed inaugurated, what precisely is to be learnt at the constitutional level? Because if, as was argued, the asymmetry that is key to 'uploading' from national to transnational is structural, and constitutive, then the learning processes can only take the form of market adjustment. In any case, and whatever the lessons to be gleaned, our reference to 'constitutional fragmentation' aimed to identify an asymmetry that is constitutive of the logic of extraction of surplus value under conditions of globalisation, and thus structural. The problem is that the generalisation of the political beyond the nation-state, the move from national to transnational politics, is significantly impacted upon, if not actually organised, by the economic logic it will then be called on to mitigate. The different logics of political and economic systems, whose own autonomy and reciprocal performance are seen

---

[45] At the transnational level, 'proportionality' becomes the way in which, sometimes explicitly, more often implicitly, a logic of accommodation, or at least balancing, is invoked to cover over the sacrifice of social rights and public value to entrepreneurial freedom. Even in the most blatant cases of such sacrifice, a language of accommodation prevails: 'Since the [Union] has thus not only an economic but also a social purpose, the rights under the provisions of the Treaty on the free movement of goods, persons, services and capital must be balanced against the objectives pursued by social policy, which include, as is clear from the first paragraph of Article [151 TFEU], inter alia, improved living and working conditions, so as to make possible their harmonisation while improvement is being maintained, proper social protection and dialogue between management and labour' (Viking *ITWF v Viking Line* (C-438/05) [2007] E.C.R. I-10779; [2008] C.M.L.R. 51 at [79]). While the wording here suggests that the economic face of the European Union (free movement of goods, persons, services, and capital) and its social dimension are potentially in conflict, it is nonetheless possible – and indeed desirable – to balance the two. Balance requires both a pivot and a metric in order to establish relative weights, a plain of commensurability on which an equilibrium may be sought.

as that which maintain differentiation, is arguably undercut at the transnational level since the political system at that level does not replicate the logic of state action, but instead, the economic system, having successfully harnessed the state to a system of global competition, simply 'exploits' it in the direction of its own aggressive expansion.

The Problem of Inclusion

One of the earliest texts to put to query the simple elevation of functional differentiation to the global scale was Marcelo Neves' important argument that in the capitalist world's 'periphery' the autopoiesis of law is best understood as an 'allopoiesis' (Neves, 2001). Luhmann's *Grundrechte*, as we saw, had placed the emphasis on *all* functional subsystems pursuing the 'inclusion of the overall population within the relevant social sphere' while supporting their 'autonomisation' (1965, 134). Neves argued that Luhmann's individual does not travel well in the world periphery, where functional differentiation had not already facilitated the smooth passage between fields of his inclusion. The periphery is not functionally differentiated, argued Neves, and as a result it harbours 'expanded and intensified' forms of exclusion.

The objection was levelled against Luhmann's optimistic assertion of the gradual, if not always smooth, world-societal development of differentiated legal and political subsystems. In later work Luhmann did concede regional exceptions to his sweeping hypothesis, societies where functional differentiation is only rudimentary and, as a result, interactional systems operating through personal ties and networks compensate for the inclusion-deficit. In fact, said Luhmann, in the periphery (and he had the favelas in Brazil and the streets of Mumbai in his sights) operates a 'meta-code' of inclusion/exclusion; the 'worst imaginable scenario will be that the society of the next century will have to accept this', and that 'the negative integration of exclusions will compete with the positive integration of inclusions' (Luhmann, 1997, 76). But this is not, objects Neves, 'about a mild meta-difference of inclusion and exclusion ... but rather about the generalised phenomenon of exclusion that questions and threatens functional differentiation, the autonomy of law and constitutional normativity' (Neves, 2001, 261), releasing and generalising destructive consequences in the periphery. And if it is the case that exclusion does unleash such tendencies, what does it mean to hold on to the promise of functional differentiation as a global phenomenon, and what does it imply to hold on to its 'primacy'?

We will have to postpone the answer to this question. Remaining closer to home, Luhmann suggested that the problem of inclusion 'can already be observed in Europe, and it is not unrealistic to expect demographic developments and migrations will feed this kind of [de-]differentiation' (1997, 76). And while it would be anachronistic to put this question to him, we might add: what does it mean to hold on to functional differentiation in the context of the financial crisis that wrecked national economies in recent times? This was a crisis that was structural, because, as Hauke Brunkhorst puts it well, the capitalist economy 'if not regulated and institutionalized appropriately' leads to a 'new kind of class rule' (Brunkhorst, 2011, 146). Brunkhorst deploys a critical reading of Luhmann to argue that:

> The social and political success of the national states depended on their ability to exclude inequalities . . . [But] the social and systemic integrative potential of the modern *world society* does not suffice to guarantee equal access to everybody. (2011, 159–60)

and later, to add:

> Whereas the national state loses its ability to exclude inequalities effectively, there is no coercive power, no sufficient administrational mechanism to implement and enforce the exclusion of the inequalities on a global, or at least a regional, level. (2011, 168–9)

To summarise, integration of the population in the functional differentiation of systems is a key premise of the tradition of social analysis that is inaugurated in Durkheim's writing on 'organic solidarity' and reaches Luhmann via Parsons. But the premise of such differentiation is the partial (differentiated) inclusion of *everyone* in those systems. That was the principle of inclusion that provided the justificatory basis in Luhmann's early *Grundrechte*: the economic subsystem depends on everyone producing and consuming, the political system on generalised citizen participation, the legal system on everyone being able to sue another, and so forth. The effects of the capitalist system in late modernity, which became so blatantly evident during the crisis, involved the creation of a privileged 'over-included' class and a class of those whose life-chances diminished to the point where their participation in society was rendered vacuous, and with it arose the spectre of exclusion of vast swathes of the world's populations from meaningful participation in social life. Which is also to say this: that the *inclusionary* propensity of rights depends heavily on their being mobilised within the regime whose production they are called to regulate, and distributions to sanction. This complementarity of rights and economic interests, as secured by the global regimes that variably fall under 'democratic capitalism', also sets the limits of the supposedly inclusive gestures performed in the functionally differentiated global setting, at the expense of those who the global system needs as neither producers nor consumers.

The Problem of Normativity

In his 1971 essay 'Die Weltgesellschaft', Luhmann argued that globalisation, or as he put it at the time the emergence of 'world society', will gradually lead to a comprehensive displacement of normative expectations by cognitive expectations, and the reliance on law and politics that once enjoyed a certain 'evolutionary and functional primacy' in societies will be replaced by a primacy of science and technology. The same urgent concern appears two decades later, as Luhmann describes the rapid shift away from expectations that are held to counterfactually and are instead forced to 'learn' in global society, and the repercussion of this shift for the function of the legal system in the face of the 'constant stream of disappointments' to which law is 'constantly called to adjust' (2004, 468). The problem of normativity is that 'world society' ushers in a significant structural shift that generates pressure on normative expectations to mutate comprehensively into cognitive expectations. Luhmann predicted that between the two types of expectation, normative and cognitive, there would be both a displacement and a blurring. A displacement to the extent that, with the advent of world society, normative expectations are guaranteed less and less by a functionally differentiated legal system; and a blurring to the extent that any clear primacy afforded to normative expectations by the legal system comes under pressure to adapt and to 'learn', and of course, to learn from disappointment is precisely what normative expectations do *not* do. Unlike cognitive expectations, which are discredited when they are disappointed, normative expectations are held on to counterfactually (see footnote 15). For example, there would be no meaning to the normativity of an expectation that one's dignity will not be violated, if every time a worker was subjected to degrading treatment they 'learnt' from the degradation and shifted their expectation. What is true of all normative expectations applies to legal expectations par excellence. By the time we reach the level of the constitution, the normative hold ought to have been strengthened significantly: at the constitutional level, normative expectations are normatively expected, sanctioned in terms of rigidity, entrenchment, and the axiomatic assertion of constitutional value.

But all this yields under the structural drift of globalisation. Increasingly, the way in which we are invited to think about the global constitution is no longer in terms of collective will-formation but instead of 'post-constituent power' (Thornhill, 2014) and to experiment with changing constituencies and networks. If in the social dimension of the constitution this move away from the logic of democratic, constituent self-determination already marks a sea change, globalisation also ushers in a high *temporal* instability in norm structures. Hartmut Rosa's famous thesis on the 'de-synchronisation' between political time – the time it takes to reach collective decisions – and the needs of market societies to respond in real time to the signals of the market, offers a critique of dialogic forms of democratic theory, the main thrust of which is that they neglect the temporal preconditions of democracy and therefore fail to grasp the current crisis of democratic self-determination under the acceleration of globalisation and the 'contraction of the present' that it ushers in (Rosa, 2005). But if the constitutional achievement comes under severe pressure in the social and temporal dimensions, it also comes under strain in the material dimension, where the constitutional thematic is increasingly withdrawn behind algorithmic governance, 'digital constitutionalism', the technologies and intraransparencies that come to underpin the new constitutionalism. The problem at the heart of this is 'finding legal forms which are compatible with the autopoiesis of law, with its specific function and the peculiarity of its coding' (Luhmann, 2004, 473), its capacity in other words to translate the demands placed upon it into its own concepts, in particular as the law increasingly adopts 'an incremental approach which depends largely on incidental events and tries to solve issues unsystematically' (Luhmann, 2004, 473).

Something of an unprecedented risk that appears now as law's 'own risk'[46] is the risk of weakening or undercutting its own reflexive intelligence, furnished by the concepts and linkages by means of which it *holds itself* at the level of internal consistency *against* the patterns of environmental complexity it discerns outwith it and selectively calls itself to manage. Luhmann's final word on law navigates tensions, paradoxes, varieties of differentiation, and dynamics of exclusion and inclusion, and it might be read as suggesting that these forms of selectivity and selective visibility are productive for law if they can counter global law's own risk, of the collapse of normativity into comprehensive learning and rapid adaptation to markets. Against the risk of fragmentation, the vast and devastating exclusions, and the loss of normativity, systems theorists have returned to redefine the function, the performance, and – crucially for constitutionality – reflexion for global law. In short, if complexity is to be navigated and managed, it must be managed in the direction of maintaining reflexivity, *eigenvalues, eigen-dynamics, and autopoiesis* as constitutively tied

---

[46] Importantly, in the tension between the two types of expectation, Luhmann read a *risk* that he saw the law of global society as being called to confront, and in confronting to assume as its own. Now, it would be misleading to suggest that Luhmann is overly worried about such mutations: if cognitive expectations flood in to fill the gap of what used to be a matter of political decision, the shrinkage of politics, to some extent, places it conveniently out of harm's way. And yet he insisted against all those who call for rethinking the function of law as having shifted *altogether* to cognitive expectations and the coordinating processes of market adjustment, that the law *must* at its core build on normative expectations. Some have read a 'normative turn' in systems theory into these imperatives.

to the function of stabilising expectations through *law's own use* of normativity, which is what the term 'constitutional' is meant to designate.

Tentative Solutions

We might identify two routes along which theories of global law provide responses to the challenges (fragmentation, exclusion, loss of normativity) that face the upscaling of the institution of law to the transnational or planetary level. The first involves reconceptualising the institution itself, stretching the 'institutional imagination', as it were,[47] renegotiating its unity: these are operations at the level of what we have called *reflexion*. The second involves reconceptualising the relation between the institution of law and the political and economic systems, rethinking the coupling and articulations between systems: these are observations that look at what we have called *performance*. It is under these two headings that we will explore the ample accommodations of global law, both their promise and their shortfall.

Reflexion: Intra-Systemic 'Solutions'

Key to renegotiating the unity of the system is to look at *constitutional function* at the global level, since, as we have emphasised throughout, it is the constitution that sustains the unity of the legal system. At one end of the spectrum we encounter the sceptics, theorists who suggest that conceptions of the constitution that entail and promote genuinely associative bonds amongst citizens cannot travel beyond the confines of the nation-state. Global constitutionalism in any but the most anaemic forms is unthinkable, because the bonds of solidarity that sustain citizenship are weakened or eroded when they are transferred to supra-state contexts. We might take Thomas Nagel's influential article on 'the problem of global justice' (2005) as a case in point. In it he argues that the 'circumstances of justice' presuppose a 'commonly authorised sovereign power' that is lacking in our globalising world. Where the requisite political structures are absent – absent in other words the conditions of political constitutionalism – the conditions of any robust sense of economic justice are similarly absent. Nagel borrows from Rawls the notion of the 'political conception' of justice to argue that the function cannot be sustained at the supranational level, that it lacks the mechanisms for collective will-formation necessary for the determination of the common good. If (re)distributive justice cannot be uploaded to the transnational level, it is because at that level there is no constitution to sanction the political-public conception of the common good.

---

[47] See Unger (1996) for this formulation, and his useful heuristic of 'mapping and criticism'.

Where such constitutional processes at state level yield forms of collective self-binding that impose duties on citizens, at the transnational level such duties can only be conceptualised as incidental costs of the interaction of actors in world markets. Thinking of the processes as isomorphic simply produces conceptual incoherence for Nagel. 'If one takes this political view, one will not find the absence of global justice a cause for distress' (2005, 121).

The 'organisation of irresponsibility' is the formulation that Scott Veitch used, so insightfully, to capture the 'legitimation of human suffering' and the kind of ethical absolution that is delivered through institutional design (Veitch, 2007). But, overall, such gestures of absolution like Nagel's[48] are not the prevailing attitudes. For the most part, theorists have been eager to embrace conceptions of the global law to address the injustice of global distributions, and we will briefly outline some of the more familiar of these in what follows. If thinking about 'global law' is mediated by the constitution, it is not only because 'the debate within global-constitutional law can be treated as a microcosm of the broader controversy over global law' (Walker, 2014, 143) but also because it is ultimately the constitution that harbours 'reflexion' as it directs 'performance', the latter in terms of the more stable and durable forms of the coupling of law with its environment.

The most pervasive development is the reconceptualisation of global constitutionalism as *global governance.* Prominent amongst the advocates here, Anne-Marie Slaughter writes of 'disaggregated statehood' governmental functions that can be performed by a number of regulatory agencies, pragmatically invested in the operation of decentralised networks of legislation, regulation, and adjudication. Significantly for Slaughter, this networked governance is not devoid of 'constitutional norms' located at the level of a 'hypothetical global polity' (Slaughter, 2005, 27–31). Dense forms of transnational regulation extend the regulatory fabric across an ever-increasing field of application, turning to problems that can be managed (but usually not resolved), where 'coalitions of interest', networks, and interstate parties engage in processes of global reach, and where jurisdictional powers and allocations are forever renegotiated. 'Stake-holding' is what both mobilises the operations of governance and is staked on them, and in the frequent references to 'reflexive', and so forth, stake-holding is what makes governance 'experimental' and, allegedly, democratic.

Distinct from governance, which is inevitably a top-down affair, even when graced with the qualification 'experimental', are 'bottom-up' aspirational solutions that locate constitutionalism at the grassroots level and theorise its

---

[48] On this, see the devastating critique of 'Nagel's Atlas' by AJ Julius (2006).

manifestations 'from below'.[49] The emphasis here is on spontaneous expressions of constitution-making that find institutional expression only approximately in the existing forms. The aspiration behind these dynamic moments, which are assumed to overflow their institutionalisation, locates the global constitution as an always-imperfect realisation of deeper dynamics. Frequently such theories, when self-identifying as 'cosmopolitan', attach to discursive-democratic processes of decision-making writ large, transferring the 'co-implication' of democracy and rights, as famously expounded by Habermas, *upward*, from national to supranational constituencies. And while these solutions often fall short of claiming 'global' incidence, they have been nevertheless highly influential in furnishing a constitutional imaginary beyond the state.

But perhaps the two most influential readings of global law arise around the 'global model of human rights' and the 'ethic of cosmopolitanism'. They aspire to strike a balance between national-constitutional understandings and global-level concepts and commitments respectively.

In the case of the former theory of global law (the 'global model of human rights'), constitutional understandings at more local levels are *reiterations*, understood as 'determinations' of the abstract concepts as more particularised conceptions.[50] This is less a 'pyramidal' structural account of law than a dialectical account, where global concepts and local variations stand in a reciprocal relation of mutual learning and adaptation. Walker puts it well when he speaks of 'rights as becoming a key *global index* of legally recognised relations, a broad plateau rather than a narrow peak' (2014, 77), where recognition takes the form of a dialectical relationship. The same broad idea has received a number of important iterations in terms of the dialectic between generalisation and re-specification of human rights.[51] Theories of proportionality aspire to realise optimal specifications of rights in particular contexts, and the widely practiced recognition of a 'margin of appreciation' also accommodates the specification of rights in national contexts in EU jurisprudence.

In the case of the latter theory of global law, a *cosmopolitan ethic* is expressed in constitutional commitments not at the level of institutional architecture but at the 'deeper level' of normative principle where they are expressed as participatory capacity, public reason, rights-protection, and so forth. The language of

---

[49] The work of Boaventura de Sousa Santos is paradigmatic here. See indicatively de Sousa Santos (2015).

[50] For the concept/conception distinction in law see Dworkin (1986, 70–2) and in philosophical literature Mulhall (2001).

[51] See Teubner (2011a) for the dialectic; see also Möller (2012). The most influential work on rights from the angle of proportionality is Alexy (2002).

'sedimentation' is evocative here, implying a historical layering of constitutional practice, though the same idea informs the 'cosmopolitan order' of rights adjudication.[52]

Under the rubric of 'cosmopolitanism', it is constitutional *pluralism* that offers the most direct affront to the theorisation of the constitutional order as unitary, arguing instead for a reflexive accommodation of constitutionalism away from unity and towards plurality. We might identify two variants here. A *first*, influential form of constitutional pluralism assumes a pluralisation of *levels*; and it comes with the production of 'decisively non-holistic forms of constitutionalism', as Walker puts it, in which constitutional norms are produced at varying levels (Walker, 2010). A *second* form involves the pluralisation of constitutional *registers* at the transnational level as pertaining to different *functional spheres* of transnational exchange and interaction; as a result, we have constitutionalisms of the 'economic', 'political', 'legal', social', 'security', and so forth varieties.[53] The division of labour is 'functional' in the sense that in each case the *sectoral* constitution is constitutively oriented to meeting the exigencies of the regulation at the transnational level of the economy, the lifeworld, of politics, or of security, whatever the field. In that sense, the proliferation of constitutional registers involves the separation of, for example, the 'economic constitution' and the 'social constitution' from the 'political constitution'.

The paradigmatic shift to constitutional pluralism *loosens the grip of normativity*; the constitution gone global is treated as an opportunity for new voices, new themes, and new arrangements to enter the scene, carried in the inflationary idiom of the 'new' constitutionalisms. For pluralists, keen to keep constitutional semantics abreast of the rapid flows of global exchange, the theoretical task becomes the breathless pursuit of 'relevance', an openness expressed in the willingness to learn and to adjust. This is 'constituent power' for the neoliberal age: pluralism is the term to which constitutional theory turns to replenish its depleted political energies, away from the older definitions and hierarchisation of priorities and commitments, the many trappings of state-'constituted' power. The loss of normativity is never anything but a gain in terms of cognition; any counter-suggestion becomes a sign of outdated theory, redundant semantics, intransigence, or naivety. And if the objection is raised that constitutional pluralism must fix at some level what is constitutional about the plurality it introduces, the response is typically to remain reflexive about that question too.

---

[52] For the theory of cosmopolitan constitutionalism see Kumm (2013); for the 'cosmopolitan order' of courts see Stone-Sweet (2012); for the layering/sedimentation idea see Tuori (2011), who also uses the term 'deep culture' to convey the same idea.

[53] See Tuori and Tuori (2014) for a significant formulation.

Set against the well-defined and highly hierarchised nested neoliberal asymmetries – the domination of the economy over collective life, of the market over any concept of the political economy, of finance over production, of services over industry, and so forth – the emancipatory gains of constitutional pluralism, by all credible accounts, have been trifling.

But such objections rarely trouble the pluralists. Against the intransigence of 'dated' formalisms, the constitutional question has now been 'answered', in large no longer beholden to the concept of the unity of law. The storming of traditional 'unitary' constitutional imaginaries by constitutional pluralism suggests removing the old fixities and leads to a renegotiation of constituencies, competencies, and structures. The notion of a constitutional project in-the-making has been greatly facilitated by the notion of *constitutionalisation* as ongoing, at which point the coupling becomes mutually productive: pluralism gains its point of purchase in constitutionalisation, which imports openness to the future, and constitutionalisation gains its justification from its ability to accommodate the plural. The becoming-constitutional comes to dominate the new space and imaginary.

And if global law indeed 'indicates a new mood' because it 'registers as a state of contestable becoming rather than corrigible achievement' (Walker, 2014, 27), let it be interjected that the intimation of global law and its attendant pluralisms strain against an understanding of the constitution as an achievement of the *unity* of legal system – a unity that serves to stabilise expectations with the promise that they will be protected, that violations of the law are not already renewals of it, that disappointments do not discredit constitutional expectations. Corrigibility has a key role to play here, as has the notion that the constitution provides the authoritative 'last word'. At one level, the distinction between normative and cognitive expectations is staked on this 'corrigibility'. If there is something vital in attempting to rescue constitutional development from its mutation to optimal market adjustment, then there is also an argument about tempering the panegyric endorsements of pluralism, and to point out the conceptual difficulties that attend its definition. This is a concern over whether (and under what conditions) we are able to hold on to the signifier 'constitutional' in the new dispensation, and to hold on to the normativity that attaches to 'political constitutionalism', not as the necessary 'drift' that accompanies globalisation, but as setting the conditions of what it might mean to carry the 'constitutional' to the transnational level.

It might be an obvious point to make at this stage, but relatively settled institutional questions of statal law become controversial, and areas of law considered relatively peripheral acquire a new centrality. The latter applies to not only the obvious case of the new prominence of international law (as quasi-global law) but also the nodal position that fields like international private law come to occupy in the new distribution of legalities, recast now in the language of 'conflicts of laws' (Joerges et al., 2011) or even 'regime-collisions' (Fischer-Lescano & Teubner, 2003). With regard to the institutional architecture itself, what HLA Hart identified as 'secondary' rules of recognition and adjudication become unsettled, and the 'paradox' of his theory that under ordinary conditions remained relatively untroubling – that those (judges) who are called to the task of recognition must also recognise the rules that define their capacity to do so – becomes a 'live' problem in the new fractious relationship between legal orders and jurisdictions that throws the neat architecture out of joint. These profound challenges inform the dilemmas that animate global law as a question of what we identified as *reflexion* and thus receive tentative answers in terms of its own, very particular intelligence.

Performance: Inter-Systemic 'Solutions'

The emphasis on performance allows us to understand how global law organises the interconnectedness between the legal system and its surrounding systems under conditions of globalisation. We look at what 'solutions' (1–4) have been offered for sustaining the articulation between the legal, economic, and political rationalities at global level.

(1) The first way to understand the interconnectedness involves downplaying the political dimension of the constitution. Cut off from any constitutive link from the political system, the reproduction of global law henceforth draws exclusively on the *deep grammar of legality*. If constitutionalism has been traditionally cast across the distinction between constituent (political) and constituted (legal) power, this first solution involves the severing of the constitutional achievement of global law from its democratic-political dimension and returning it to law's very own resources, as it were. Thereafter, global law is no longer about giving legal expression to democratic imperatives, but simply reproducing its internal values of coherence, publicity, generality, transparency, and so forth, without recourse to political processes as a source of input or legitimation. It may be straining the notion of the 'inter-systemic' to extend it to describe the *absence* of relation, but it is nonetheless on this absence (of democratic redress) that global law scores one of its most enduring successes. The solution it offers is to remove from global law the need to legitimise itself in terms of input and democratic credentials.

The exponential spread of 'global administrative law' (GAL) is a case in point. Relieved of the need to legitimise its operation in terms of democratic input, sites of transnational regulation and decision-making have emerged under the umbrella notion of GAL, exercising 'authority of the type traditionally associated with the public authority of the state' but now 'in circumstances where states either play no part in the generation of norms, or where the link with the original authority of the state has been radically attenuated or lost' (Walker, 2014, 103).[54] Lost also is any sense in which this rapidly expanding area of transnational law depends on democratic input, pedigree, or credentials. What it draws its legitimation from, instead, are the virtues of *legality*[55] by professing a distinctive quality of publicness and due process. As its more famous advocate puts it, it is concerned with the tasks of 'channelling, managing, shaping and constraining political power' (Kingsbury, 2009, quoted in Walker, 2014, 105), where the channelling, and so forth, in turn invokes reason-giving, accountability and proportionality, and the qualities traditionally associated with the normative value of legality.

(2) *Societal constitutionalism* involves a very different solution to the inter-systemic relation, and with it a different basis of legitimation.[56] In Teubner's powerful formulation of the notion, his solution to the asymmetry he described for us earlier between the propulsion of the economic system to the global level and the political and legal systems lagging behind is not to attempt to reconceive the latter at the global level but to abandon the idea that the State can serve as the vehicle for a political society's self-organisation. The inaugurating move of societal constitutionalism involves the severing of the 'constitutional' from the 'statal' and its return in 'capillary' form. Similarly to the tendency described immediately above, the *constituent* dimension of constitutionalism recedes here, and yet it is not abandoned, as with the first solution, but reconceptualised as 'a communicative potential', a 'type of social energy', a 'pulsating process' (2012, 62, 63) that subtends and animates a series of 'capillary constitutions' of transnational society, which organise various functional spheres of society into an *acentric* order and frame the question of collective action as appropriate to each of them. These fields, which harbour lasting structures for particular sets of exchanges, include of course the economy but also the global educational and communication sectors, all the way to the regulation of the internet, the arts, sport, and so forth.

---

[54] Examples include the regulatory activities of the WHO; transnational financial networks like the Basle Comtee of heads of central banks; public/private hybrids like ICANN; international sport's anti-doping agency, and so forth (see Walker, 2014).

[55] In the way perhaps that Lon Fuller understood the 'inner morality of law' in his highly influential *The Morality of Law* (1964).

[56] For a recent account see Golia and Teubner (2021).

The assumption, and promise, is that with the new societal form of 'self-constitutionalisation of global orders', their dependency on 'the power of states, state policies and the ideologies of political parties' will abate, and societal constitutions will be tightly coupled to 'interest constellations within the global fragments' instead. While this may well 'result in a greater responsiveness to social needs than the constitutional law laid down by state authorities' (2012, 54), since it is decentralised collective actors that shape the order of the various domains (122), the risk is that an excessively close coupling of societal constitutions to 'partial interests' may lead to 'corrupt' constitutional norms. It remains to be seen, he says, whether countervailing influences from institutions and civil society will balance out the risk of corruption. This is an important question to which his *Constitutional Fragments* lends significant insight in a number of respects. The one that concerns us here is the particular insight into the potential inherent in the capillary constitutions of balancing their autonomy while reining in expansionist tendencies of any one of the subsystems (see in particular Teubner, 2011a). In an argument that updates Luhmann's *Grundrechte*, Teubner analyses *fundamental rights* as setting boundaries to totalising tendencies of function systems, and their value in this respect is that they are protective against the 'endangerment of individuals' integrity of body and mind by a multiplicity of anonymous, autonomised and today globalized communicative processes' (Teubner, 2011b, 144). Teubner's (2012) approach in is to ask whether a sufficiently large degree of external pressure might push subsystems into self-*limitation*. The intention is to track the possibility of reflexive readjustment on the part of each system's 'internal constitution', with the emphasis on self-limitation, expressed in terms of 'self-discipline', aimed at countering each system's 'imperialist' tendency to grow. The focus thus shifts from the constitutive to the limitative. It refers no longer to the question: what are the institutional preconditions of the autonomy of functional subsystems? It refers rather to the question: where are the limits of their expansion, before their expansionist tendencies 'tip [them] into destructive-ness?' (2012, 75) Also, much of the concern now has, understandably, shifted away from the expansionism of the legal and political systems, tracked as 'juridification' and 'politicisation' in earlier work, towards the *economy*.

As in older writings on 'reflexive law', the emphasis is again on self-steering, and the challenge is to combine 'external pressures with internal processes of discovery' to enable such steering. It used to be the case that the problem was the state superimposing its rationality to attempt to achieve results;[57] now it is

---

[57] Teubner's warning that 'following the experiences of political totalitarianism in the last century, a permanent subordination of the subsystems to the state is no longer a valid option' (2011a, 13).

the economy. And while 'high cognitive demands' will be made of 'national and international interventions by the world of states', especially in a situation of economic crisis, the temptation must be resisted to substitute their – the states' – reason for that of the focal system, here the economy. Instead, their intervention should consist in the 'selective' generation of 'constitutional irritants' that will translate into self-steering, that will liberate systems from pathologies in the form of 'self-blockades' but not super-impose state rationality. Hence, there is 'no alternative but to experiment with constitutionalisation', in the hope that 'with a bit of luck' 'the external and internal programmes' – of irritating and irritated systems – 'will 'play out together along the desired course' (2011a, 15).

(3) A decade after his critique of the functionally differentiated legal system as harbouring 'expanded and intensified' forms of exclusion when it came to the 'periphery', Marcelo Neves' theorising of *trans-constitutionalism* revisits the argument about exclusion on the global scale, as an argument about pathologies of differentiation. He describes the 'hypertrophic growth' of the economic system against 'the atrophic propensity' of the legal and political systems (2013, 33). With the balance thrown off-kilter, functional differentiation does not hold. This leads to 'systemic corruption', which leaves the legal system incapable of self-reproduction and operative closure. The diagnosis: the mechanism of structural coupling that maintained stable patterns of mutual conditioning between systems comes asunder with the *corruption* of the constitution, with the effect that the economic system colonises the field. Economic efficiency becomes the 'contingency formula' for both politics and law, displacing their own 'contingency formulae' of justice and legitimacy respectively; reciprocal *performance* is replaced by unidirectionality; even *reflexion* – Luhmann's term for systemic self-reference – is colonised, with economic thinking transplanted into the way that the law 'thinks'. Constitutionality at that point is floated across stretches of equivalence made possible by the wholesale export of economic metrics and semantics to other fields. Trans-constitutionalism expresses the 'normative turn' in systems theory in the insistence that 'constitutional normativity' not be lost at the global level, but rather deployed, for Neves, in the form of a *transversal rationality*. The emphasis is on functional analysis as problem-centred analysis: it begins with a trans-constitutional *problem* and seeks solutions across the many levels – national, international, supranational, and so forth – at which constitutional iterations are available. Transversal rationality is an attempt to sustain at the global level something of the normative function of the constitution where the more 'lasting, stable and concentrated' forms of structural coupling are no longer available (2013, 26), but where different 'bridges of transition' might offer passage between autonomous spheres (both *within* multilevel legalities and *across* systemic boundaries)

and new opportunities to adapt the semantics of the constitution to changing structures, since the requirement of any agreed content is no longer a condition of successful communication.

Function, again, is central here, and as in all functional analysis one begins with the question: what is the problem to which the constitution is the answer? In Neves' iteration of the functional argument, the constitution at the reflexive level functions to balance systemic complexity with social heterogeneity so that the former is adequate to the latter. 'In the case of the transversal constitution the link occurs between two structural reflexive mechanisms: on the one hand the legal constitution as a set of norms of norms; and on the other hand the political constitution as a ... decision-making process binding decision-making processes. This reflexive transversality enables learning [across the two] to be intensified' (2013, 43). The analysis is complex and aims to keep transnational legal operations within the constitutional key, and with it something of the normative concept of the constitution alive. If, with the migration to the global level, constitutionalism might need to be 're-signified', the relationship between semantics and structures rethought, the most difficult question that needs to be answered is how to rescue a concept of the constitution from the shifting sands of globalisation, and Neves' 'trans-constitutionalism' attempts to achieve this at the level of the coupling of the systems at the reflexive level.

(4) The final global-constitutional solution that we visit involves the suggestion that the law, specifically legal rights, perform a new *meta*function at the global level, understood as a *'super-coding' of political power*. The analysis draws from Luhmann's posthumously published treatise on the political system (Luhmann, 2015). Earlier he had identified the constitutional function as providing stable forms of coupling between subsystems. In the later work, and in terms of reiterating his message against attributing heightened significance to the political system, Luhmann proposes a special role for rights. *Rights*, he argues, offer a *second-coding of the political system* itself. His earlier analyses of rights, remember, defended them as vehicles of inclusion (in the variety of functional domains) and as buttressing the unchecked excesses of political power. Now, in *Politische Soziologie* (2015) something significantly novel is offered because legal rationality, expressed in rights, undergirds the political system's very possibility of performing its function, no longer simply in the expectation that its addressees will be legal subjects, but further suggesting that the political system can only effectively exercise political power if it is vested as legal power (i.e. as lawful power). The political form of that exercise is constitutively legal; and if this intimates an unusual departure from the way he had earlier invited us to think of the radical closure of systems around their self-reference, so be it. Now, as Chris Thornhill puts it well, 'political power relies on the presence of a systemically (not reflexively)

generalised rationality to perform its functions' (2018, 130). The distinction intimates this: that if political power now needs to be legally generalised, the conditions of its exercise require something outside its own rationality to direct it, in other words outside what it can reflexively achieve on its own (on the basis of the distinction that as code underlies it).

As Thornhill describes it:

> What is striking in the transformation of modern democracy is that *the law itself* produces authority for democratic norms, and many ideally political sources of norm construction have been supplanted by concepts that are internal to the law: *the legal system itself, in its globally overarching form, becomes the subject that underlies democracy*, and there is no external political subject to support the law. This is especially striking in the essential political form of the constitution, which, in most societies, simply results from inner-legal acts. Indeed, *the law itself widely internalizes the classical functions of citizenship.* (Thornhill, 2018, 209–10)

Thornhill's own suggestion, developed in a number of recent works, rehearses and strengthens this internal dependency of the political to the legal system, which in many respects involves a process of *surrogation*. Democracy may have burst onto the scene of modernity in terms of the exercise of constituent power and in the guise of collective self-legislation, but any adequate understanding of it today, argues Thornhill, will cede the primacy to the constituted, rather than the constituent, side. 'Contemporary democracy is built around *functional equivalents* to classical patterns of democratic citizenship, and these equivalents are primarily constructed within the law: law's reference to law emerges as an equivalent to classical concepts of political voluntarism and subjectivity'. He concludes: 'The primary level of norm construction – that is, the construction of the basic and irreducible residue of legitimacy – occurs within the global legal system, expressed through equivalents to political will-formation' (210). Unlike the 'deep grammar of legality' of the earlier solution (1), the emphasis here is not on eclipsing but on *internalising* constituent power, by providing functional equivalents to its exercise. The effect of this metalevel juridification, is to harness the exercise of democratic self-determination to regimes of rights, thereby collapsing constituent power into the limited and limiting domain of global opportunities of the deployment of rights.

4 Conclusion

We have come a long way since we spoke of the emergence and consolidation of functional differentiation in early modern history. We began by looking at the theoretical orientation of social theory to differentiation that was inaugurated in

Durkheim's 'division of labour'. It finds its definitive restatement as *functional* differentiation in Parsons' theory of the structure of social action (Parsons, 1937). It is in Luhmann's work that the theory of functional differentiation finds its radical restatement with the shift from action to communication as the focus of the sociological perspective, and with its decisive reorientation to the question of time. This move will relieve sociology from the overstated and projected homogeneities of shared culture and core moral values that were there to buttress the 'structure of social action' and invite it instead as a question of complexity. The dynamic of differentiation ties to the *stabilising* function of law, which at the same time performs an important further role in guarding against the danger of de-differentiation on the one side and of entropy and societal breakdown on the other. Fundamental constitutional rights, it was argued, have a key role to play here.

That functional differentiation involved the rationalisation of spheres of activity on the basis of specialised functions leads to an increase in complexity in the differentiated spheres that the adequate performance of that function makes necessary. A careful architecture of mutual performances organises the field of functional differentiation, with demands placed on the reflection of systems in terms of self-limitation and the maintenance of proper boundaries. If the new rationalities of the economy, of politics, of the range of differentiated spheres, remain meaningful in this precarious dispensation, it is because as differentiated they discipline the double contingency of action that would otherwise spell meaninglessness. Differentiation is experienced as inclusion in functional spheres, and as the proponents of differentiation (Durkheim, Parsons, Luhmann) would have it, it delivers the dividends of a flourishing, multifaceted agency. At the same time, as we saw, the careful architecture of functional rationalities was from the start of the project of modernity super-coded to capitalist conditions, operations, and distributions. Differentiation ensured the smooth running of the economy on the basis of its own values and modalities in the advanced capitalist economies of the metropolitan centres of commerce and industry, without the need to exercise political power to ensure social reproduction and the perpetuation of the system, while in periphery the operation of capitalism combined with the violent, extractive colonial economy.

In Section 2 of the Element, we saw how the careful architecture of differentiation, balance, and mutual performance was jeopardised, with the hypertrophy of any one of the structurally coupled systems at the expense of the others. The pathologies were described by the terms 'juridification', 'politicisation', and 'marketisation'. Marketisation is the pathology most pertinent today, firstly because the market was able to 'export' the means of 'veridiction' to other systems, that is, it was able to provide a means to guide the operations of both the political and legal systems, and secondly because under conditions of globalisation, market thinking came to inform, if not organise, the architecture itself. In the process, economic reason, now clearly distinct, or *differentiated*, from its political encumbrance, is no longer set *alongside* but rather *above* other rationalities. In the process, market thinking hoists itself to the position of a privileged site of societal rationality. But, by definition, under the organising principle of functional differentiation, no functional-systemic rationality can occupy this privileged position over and above its specific functional reach.

In our discussion of globalisation, we encountered certain obvious limits to upscaling functional differentiation to the global level. It is a level at which the 'pathologies' we tracked have been in actual practice instrumentalised to maximise the returns for globally circulating capital. Fragmentation, exclusion, and the loss of political capacity (what we called the shift from normative to cognitive expectations) accompany the generalisation of economic reason to the global level. We looked at these in the final section of the Element and then briefly moved on to look at what 'solutions' might be available from the point of view of law, of what 'global law' might mean and entail. 'Solutions' bifurcated at this point into 'intra-systemic' and 'inter-systemic'. Under the first heading the focus was placed on holding on to 'global' law's autonomy and differenti-ation as a system, in which case solutions depended on holding on to the constitutional function of law as informing and subtending its own reflexive intelligence. Under the second heading we explored the capacity of 'global law' to navigate the complexity of its environment, the facilitations and blockages of globalisation. In the process it became crucial to prevent that law's reflexive intelligence from immediately folding into what Luhmann called its 'adaptive intelligence', that is, that its successful adaptation to the global economy not be the occasion of the abandonment of its own reflexive achievement. This is a 'crucial' proviso if we expect our law to hold the line against the comprehen-sive generalisation of economic reason and 'total market thinking'. A great deal is clearly staked on this, in terms of our societies' ability to fashion, and to hold on to, normative commitments and political choices that we are prepared to enshrine, and defend, as *our* democratic law.

References

Ackerman, B (1984) 'Discovering the Constitution'. *Yale Law Journal*, 93(6), 1013–72.

Alexy, R (1989) *A Theory of Legal Argumentation* (trans. R Adler and DN MacCormick). Oxford: Oxford University Press.

Alexy, R (2002) *A Theory of Constitutional Rights* (trans. J Rivers). Oxford: Oxford University Press.

Berman, HJ (2003) *Law and Revolution.* Vol. II, *The Impact of the Protestant Reformations on the Western Legal Tradition.* Cambridge, MA: Harvard University Press.

Bloch, E (2018/1986) *On Karl Marx*. London: Verso.

Brunkhorst, H (2011) 'The Return of Crisis' in P Kjaer, G Teubner and A Febbrajo (eds.), *The Financial Crisis in Constitutional Perspective.* Oxford: Hart, pp. 133–72.

Choudry, S (ed.) (2007) *The Migration of Constitutional Ideas*. Cambridge: Cambridge University Press.

Christodoulidis, E (2020) 'The Myth of Democratic Governance' in PF Kjaer (ed.), *The Law of Political Economy: Transformation in the Function of Law.* Cambridge: Cambridge University Press, pp. 62–88.

Christodoulidis, E (2021) *The Redress of Law.* Cambridge: Cambridge University Press.

Christodoulidis, E, Dukes, R and Goldoni, M (2019) *Research Handbook in Critical Legal Theory.* Cheltenham: Edward Elgar.

de Sousa Santos, B (2015) *Epistemologies of the South: Justice against Epistemicide.* London: Routledge.

Debray, R (1983) *Critique of Political Reason.* London: Verso.

Derrida, J (1992) 'Force of Law: The "Mystical Foundations of Authority"' in D Cornell, M Rosenfeld and D Gray Carson (eds.), *Deconstruction and the Possibility of Justice.* New York: Routledge, pp. 3–67.

Dobner, P and Loughlin, M (eds.) (2010) *The Twilight of Constitutionalism.* Oxford: Oxford University Press.

Durkheim, E (1893/1965) *De la division du travail social* (trans. G Simpson). London: Free Press.

Dworkin, R (1986) *Law's Empire.* London: Fontana.

Fischer-Lescano, A and Teubner, G (2003) 'Regime-Collisions: The Vain Search for Legal Unity in the Fragmentation of Global Law'. *Michigan Journal of International Law*, 25(4), 999–1046.

Foucault, M (2000) 'Governmentality' in *Essential Works of Foucault 1954–1984*. Vol. III, *Power*. New York: New Press, pp. 201–22.

Foucault, M (2004) *The Birth of Biopolitics*. New York: Palgrave Macmillan.

Fuller, LL (1964) *The Morality of Law*. New Haven, CT: Yale University Press.

Galbraith, JK (1987) *A History of Economics: The Past as the Present*. London: H. Hamilton.

Golia, A and Teubner, G (2021) 'Societal Constitutionalism: Background, Theory, Debates'. *Vienna Journal on International Constitutional Law*, 1–55.

Gorz, A (1989) *Critique of Economic Reason*. London: Verso.

Guibentif, P (2016) 'Rights in Niklas Luhmann's Systems Theory' in G Harste (ed.), *Law and Intersystemic Communication: Understanding 'Structural Coupling'*. New York: Routledge, pp. 255–88.

Habermas, J (1984) *The Theory of Communicative Action*. Cambridge: Polity Press.

Habermas, J (1995) *Between Facts and Norms*, Cambridge: Polity Press.

Habermas, J (2001) 'Constitutional Democracy: A Paradoxical Union of Contradictory Principles?' *Political Theory*, 29(6), 766–81.

Hart, HLA (1961) *The Concept of Law*. Oxford: Clarendon.

Harvey, D (2003) *The New Imperialism*. Oxford: Oxford University Press.

Joerges, C, Kjaer, PF and Ralli, T (2011) 'A New Type of Conflicts Law as Constitutional Form in the Postnational Constellation'. *Transnational Legal Theory*, 2(2), 153–65.

Julius, AJ (2006) 'Nagel's Atlas'. *Philosophy and Public Affairs*, 34(2), 176–92.

Kahn-Freund, O (1954) 'The Legal Framework' in A. Flanders and H. Clegg (eds.), *The System of Industrial Relations in Great Britain*. Oxford, Blackwell, p. 1.

Kingsbury, B (2009) 'The Concept of "Law" in Global Administrative Law'. *European Journal of International Law*, 20(1), 3–57.

Kjaer, PF (2014) *Constitutionalism in the Global Realm: A Sociological Approach*. London: Routledge.

Kumm, M (2013) 'The Cosmopolitan Turn in Constitutionalism: An Integrated Conception of Public Law'. *Indiana Journal of Global Legal Studies*, 20(2), 605–28.

Laclau, E (1996) 'Why Do Empty Signifiers Matter to Politics?' in *Emancipation(s)*. London: Verso.

Lindahl, H (2013) *Fault Fines of Globalization: Legal Order and the Politics of A-legality*. Oxford: Oxford University Press.

Loughlin M and Walker, N (eds.) (2007) *The Paradox of Constitutionalism: Constituent Power and Constitutional Form*. Oxford: Oxford University Press.

Luhmann, N (1965) *Grundrechte als Institution*. Berlin: Duncker and Humblot.

Luhmann, N (1971) 'Die Weltgesellschaft'. *Archiv für Rechts- und Sozialphilosophie/Archives for Philosophy of Law and Social Philosophy*, 57(1), 1–35.

Luhmann, N (1972) *The Sociological Theory of Law* (trans. E King-Utz and M Albrow). London: Routledge and Kegan Paul.

Luhmann, N (1982) *The Differentiation of Society* (trans. S Holmes and C Larmore). New York: Columbia University Press.

Luhmann, N (1986a) *Ecological Communication* (trans. J Bednarz). Cambridge: Polity Press.

Luhmann, N (1986b) 'The Self-Reproduction of Law and Its Limits' in G Teubner (ed.), *Autopoietic Law: A New Approach to Law and Society*. Berlin: de Gruyter, pp. 60–81.

Luhmann, N (1989) *Gesellschaftstruktur und Semantic II*. Frankfurt: Suhrkamp.

Luhmann, N (1990a) *Political Theory in the Welfare State*. Berlin: de Gruyter.

Luhmann, N (1990b) 'Verfassung als evolutionare Errungenschaft'. *Rechtshistorisches Journal*, 9, 176–220.

Luhmann, N (1995a/1984) *Social Systems* (trans. J Bednarz, Jr., with D Baecker). Stanford, CA: Stanford University Press.

Luhmann, N (1995b) 'Inklusion und Exklusion' in *Soziologische Aufklärung*. Vol. 6. Opladen: Westdeutscher Verlag, pp. 237–64.

Luhmann, N (1997) 'Globalization or World Society: How to Conceive of Modern Society?' *International Review of Sociology*, 7(1), 67–79.

Luhmann, N (2004) *Law as a Social System* (trans. K Ziegert). Oxford: Oxford University Press.

Luhmann, N (2015) *Politische Soziologie*. Frankfurt: Suhrkamp Verlag.

Lukács, G (1923/1971) *History and Class Consciousness: Studies in Marxist Dialectics* (trans. R Livingstone). London: Merlin.

MacCormick, DN (1981) *H L A Hart*. Oxford: Oxford University Press.

Malthus, T (1992/1798) *Malthus: 'An Essay on the Principle of Population'*. Cambridge: Cambridge University Press.

Marx, K (1843/2000) 'On the Jewish Question' in D. MacLellan (ed.), *Karl Marx: Selected Writings*. Oxford: Oxford University Press, pp. 46–63.

Möller, K (2012) *The Global Model of Constitutional Rights*. Oxford: Oxford University Press.

Mulhall, S (2001) *Inheritance and Originality*. Oxford: Oxford University Press.

Nagel, T (2005) 'The Problem of Global Justice'. *Philosophy & Public Affairs*, 33(2), 113–47.

Neves, M (2001) 'From the Autopoiesis to the Allopoiesis of Law'. *Journal of Law and Society*, 28(2), 242–64.

Neves, M (2013) *Transconstitutionalism*. Oxford: Bloomsbury.

Parsons, T (1937) *The Structure of Social Action*. New York: Free Press.

Polanyi, K (1944) *The Great Transformation*. Boston, MA: Beacon Press.

Rawls, J (1997) 'The Idea of Public Reason Revisited'. *University of Chicago Law Review*, 64(3), 766–807.

Roll, E (1956) *A History of Economic Thought*. London: Faber.

Rosa, H (2005) 'The Speed of Global Flows and the Pace of Democratic Politics'. *New Political Science*, 27(4), 445–59.

Rosanvallon, P (2000) *The New Social Question: Rethinking the Welfare State*. Princeton, NJ: Princeton University Press.

Savage, M (2021) *The Return of Inequality*. Cambridge, MA: Harvard University Press.

Simitis, S (1986) 'Juridification of Labor Relations'. *Comparative Labor Law*, 7(2), 93–142.

Slaughter, AM (2005) *A New World Order*. Princeton, NJ: Princeton University Press.

Stone-Sweet, A (2012) 'A Cosmopolitan Legal Order: Constitutional Pluralism and Rights Adjudication in Europe'. *Global Constitutionalism*, 1(1), 53–90.

Streeck, W (2014) *Buying Time: The Delayed Crisis of Democratic Capitalism*. London: Verso.

Supiot, A (2007) *Homo Juridicus: On the Anthropological Function of the Law* (trans. S Brown). London: Verso. (Originally Seuil, 2005.)

Supiot, A (2017) *Governance by Numbers: The Making of a Legal Model of Allegiance*. Oxford: Hart.

Supiot, A (2006) 'Law and Labour'. *New Left Review*, 39, 109–21.

Teubner, G (1983) 'Substantive and Reflexive Elements in Modern Law'. *Law & Society Review*, 17, 239–85.

Teubner, G (1987) 'Juridification: Concepts, Aspects, Limits, Solutions' in G Teubner (ed.), *Juridification of Social Spheres*. Berlin: de Gruyter, pp. 3–42.

Teubner, G (2006) 'The Anonymous Matrix: Human Rights Violations by "Private" Transnational Actors'. *Modern Law Review*, 69, 327–46.

Teubner, G (2011a) 'Constitutionalising Polycontexturality'. *Social and Legal Studies,* 20, 209–52.

Teubner, G (2011b) 'A Constitutional Moment? The Logics of "Hitting the Bottom"' in P Kjaer, G Teubner and A Febbrajo (eds.), *The Financial Crisis in Constitutional Perspective: The Dark Side of Functional Differentiation*. Oxford: Oxford University Press, pp. 9–51.

Teubner, G (2012) *Constitutional Fragments: Societal Constitutionalism and Globalization*. Oxford: Oxford University Press.

Thompson, EP (1963) *The Making of the English Working Class*. London: Vintage Books.

Thornhill, C (2006) 'Luhmann's Political Theory: Politics after Metaphysics?' in M King and C Thornhill (eds.), *Luhmann on Law and Politics*. Oxford: Hart, 75–100.

Thornhill, C (2012) 'Sociological Enlightenments and the Sociology of Political Philosophy'. *Revue internationale de philosophie*, 1, 55–83.

Thornhill, C (2016) 'On Norms as Social Facts: A View from Historical Political Science' in W. Rasch (ed.), *'Tragic Choices': Luhmann on Law and States of Exception*. Oldenbourg: De Gruyter, pp. 47–67.

Thornhill, C (2018) *The Sociology of Law and the Global Transformation of Democracy*. Cambridge: Cambridge University Press.

Tuori, K (2011) *Ratio and Voluntas: The Tension between Reason and Will in Law*. Farnham: Ashgate.

Tuori, K and Tuori, K (2014) *The Eurozone Crisis: A Constitutional Analysis*. Cambridge: Cambridge University Press.

Unger, RM (1996) 'Legal Analysis as Institutional Imagination'. *Modern Law Review*, 59(1), 1–23.

van der Walt, J (2020) *The Concept of Liberal Democratic Law*. London: Routledge.

Veitch, S (2007) *Law and Irresponsibility: On the Legitimation of Human Suffering*. London: Routledge.

Verschraegen G (2006) 'Systems Theory and the Paradox of Human Rights' in M King and C Thornhill (eds.), *Luhmann on Law and Politics*. Oxford: Hart, pp. 101–25.

Verschraegen, G (2002). 'Human Rights and Modern Society: A Sociological Analysis from the Perspective of Systems Theory'. *Journal of Law and Society*, 29(2), 258–81.

Walker, N (2002) 'The Idea of Constitutional Pluralism'. *Modern Law Review*, 65(3), 317–59.

Walker, N (2010) 'Multilevel Constitutionalism: Looking beyond the German Debate' in K Tuori and S. Sankari (eds.), *The Many Constitutions of Europe*. Farnham: Ashgate, pp. 143–68.

Walker, N (2014) *Intimations of Global Law*. Cambridge: Cambridge University Press.

Walzer, M (1983) *Spheres of Justice: A Defense of Pluralism and Equality*. New York: Basic Books.

Weber, M (1978) *Economy and Society.* Berkeley: University of California Press.

Weber, M (1946) 'Science as a Vocation'. In AI Tauber (ed.), *Science and the Quest for Reality: Main Trends of the Modern World.* London: Palgrave Macmillan, pp. 382–94.

Weber, M (2002/1905) *The Protestant Ethic and the Spirit of Capitalism.* London: Routledge.

Weil, D (2014) *The Fissured Workplace.* Cambridge, MA: Harvard University Press.

Wood, EM (1981) 'The Separation of the Economic and the Political in Capitalism'. *New Left Review,* 127, 65–95.

Cambridge Elements ⁼

Philosophy of Law

Series Editors

George Pavlakos
University of Glasgow

George Pavlakos is Professor of Law and Philosophy at the School of Law, University of Glasgow. He has held visiting posts at the universities of Kiel and Luzern, the European University Institute, the UCLA Law School, the Cornell Law School, and the Beihang Law School in Beijing. He is the author of *Our Knowledge of the Law* (2007) and more recently has co-edited *Agency, Negligence and Responsibility* (2021) and *Reasons and Intentions in Law and Practical Agency* (2015).

Gerald J. Postema
University of North Carolina at Chapel Hill

Gerald J. Postema is Professor Emeritus of Philosophy at the University of North Carolina at Chapel Hill. Among his publications count *Utility, Publicity, and Law: Bentham's Moral and Legal Philosophy* (2019); *On the Law of Nature, Reason, and the Common Law: Selected Jurisprudential Writings of Sir Matthew* Hale (2017); *Legal Philosophy in the Twentieth Century: The Common Law World* (2011), *Bentham and the Common Law Tradition*, 2nd edition (2019).

Kenneth M. Ehrenberg
University of Surrey

Kenneth M. Ehrenberg is Professor of Jurisprudence and Philosophy at the University of Surrey School of Law and Co-Director of the Surrey Centre for Law and Philosophy. He is the author of The Functions of Law (2016) and numerous articles on the nature of law, jurisprudential methodology, the relation of law to morality, practical authority, and the epistemology of evidence law.

Associate Editor

Sally Zhu
University of Sheffield

Sally Zhu is a Lecturer in Property Law at University of Sheffield. Her research is on property and private law aspects of platform and digital economies.

About the Series

This series provides an accessible overview of the philosophy of law, drawing on its varied intellectual traditions in order to showcase the interdisciplinary dimensions of jurisprudential enquiry, review the state of the art in the field, and suggest fresh research agendas for the future. Focussing on issues rather than traditions or authors, each contribution seeks to deepen our understanding of the foundations of the law, ultimately with a view to offering practical insights into some of the major challenges of our age.

Cambridge Elements ≡

Philosophy of Law

Printed in the United States
by Baker & Taylor Publisher Services